THE UNSEEN PROFESSIONAL

Product Leadership in the Midst of Bureaucracy

THE UNSEEN PROFESSIONAL

Product Leadership in the Midst of Bureaucracy

Nathaniel Dull

Published 2026

Published by Kyberno Solutions, LLC

linkedin.com/in/nathaniel-dull/

ISBN: 979-8-9953247-0-6 (paperback)

Printed in the United States of America

For my wife —

my biggest supporter, my steadiest presence,

and the reason every lily pad feels less terrifying.

And for our daughters —

may you always know that the work you love is worth doing,

even when no one is watching.

CONTENTS

INTRODUCTION

The Job Description Lied

You have delivered the projects nobody noticed. You have kept initiatives alive through budget cycles, leadership transitions, and reorganizations that had nothing to do with the work and disrupted it anyway. You have sat in rooms where the wrong priorities won, watched decisions get made for reasons that had nothing to do with the evidence, and found ways to keep moving forward anyway.

You have the skills. What you have not always had is a map. This book is that map.

The first time I stood in front of a live crew and tried to direct a church service, I nearly fell apart.

I had done the prep work. I knew the rundown. I understood the pieces: the camera operators, the lighting technicians, the stage hands, the band, the executive producer, the lyrics on the screens. What I didn't understand was how fast it would all move, how quickly one missed cue could cascade into chaos, and how little time there was to think. The pace was relentless. The pace didn't care about my confidence.

People saw me struggle. Some of them said, quietly and not so quietly, that I wouldn't be able to do it.

I kept going anyway.

That was my first real introduction to what I now know as product and project management—though nobody called it that at the time. I was a Technical Director in Chicago, orchestrating dozens of moving parts in real time, staying calm when things broke, reading the room, making split-second decisions, keeping a team of volunteers coordinated and confident. I was twenty-something years old and learning, entirely by doing, that leadership isn't a title. It's a practice.

A lot of what I learned in that role, I credit to my executive producer. She was remarkable—patient when I needed patience, demanding when I needed a push, and above all, she believed in me before I fully believed in myself. I've been lucky enough to have mentors like that throughout my career: people who saw something in me and didn't let me settle. If you have someone like that in your corner, hold onto them. If you don't have one yet, this book is partly written to be that voice.

• • •

My path from that Chicago church stage to leading enterprise product management inside the federal government wasn't a straight line. It never is. There were years in Washington DC doing installs at federal government facilities, a transition into the federal world at the Centers for Medicare and Medicaid Services, and eventually a decade-long journey managing a SharePoint portfolio that grew from something small into something that served 9,000 people, processed terabytes of data, and touched nearly every corner of one of the most complex agencies in the United States government.

Along the way, I learned something that most product management books won't tell you: the job description was never really about the job.

The job description will tell you about roadmaps, backlogs, sprint ceremonies, and stakeholder management. It will mention Agile, SAFe, Scrum. It will list the tools: Jira, Confluence, Azure DevOps. It will probably include the phrase "influence without authority," which is polite corporate language for one of the hardest things a professional can be asked to do: drive outcomes when you have no formal power over the people you need.

What the job description won't tell you is this: in a large organization (a federal agency, a healthcare system, a regulated enterprise), the real work happens in the hallways, the difficult conversations, the budget cycles, the compliance reviews, and the 115 executive briefings you'll deliver trying to keep a single initiative alive. The real work is political in the truest sense of the word. It requires patience, strategy, resilience, and a kind of calm that you have to build deliberately because it doesn't come naturally to anyone.

Nobody teaches you that in a certification course.

• • •

A Note to the Person Who Feels Behind

Before I go further, I want to speak directly to someone who may be reading this with a specific kind of anxiety—the person who wonders whether their background is enough.

Maybe you came from government and you're not sure the private sector will understand what you built. Maybe you came from a non-traditional field—production, operations, something that doesn't map cleanly onto a product management job description—and you're worried the pedigree police will catch you at the door. Maybe you're watching colleagues with fancier titles or more recognizable company names on their resumes and wondering if you're already behind in a race you didn't realize you'd entered.

I have heard this from federal workers especially, in the period when many of them found themselves unexpectedly in transition. Highly educated, deeply experienced, genuinely accomplished people who had spent years serving the public, and who were suddenly uncertain whether any of that would translate. They watched people like me navigate the crossing and asked: did you make it? Is it worth trying?

Here is what I tell them, and what I want to tell you: you are more qualified than you think. The skills you built in whatever environment formed you, the patience, the scale, the judgment, the ability to operate in complex systems, under real accountability, those things travel. They don't always come with a private sector translation pre-loaded, and part of this book is about how to build that translation. But the substance is there. It has always been there.

You were hired, somewhere, by someone, because of you—not because of a perfectly matched job description. No job description has ever remained exactly what it was when it was posted. The organization hired you because they saw something. Your job is to keep showing them they were right.

Everyone starts over. I started over. The only way to know if the next chapter works is to begin writing it.

• • •

Why This Book Exists

I've watched a lot of talented people struggle inside large organizations—not because they lacked skills, but because they lacked a map. The startup PM playbooks don't translate. The certification frameworks give you the vocabulary but not the wisdom. And the people who actually know how to navigate complex enterprise environments are often too busy navigating them to write anything down.

This book is my attempt to write it down.

There's also something bigger happening right now that I can't ignore. We are in a moment of profound transition: in technology, in work, and in the nature of organizations themselves. Artificial intelligence is changing what products look like, how teams operate, and what skills will matter in five years. People are anxious about this, and understandably so. I've been in technology for a long time, and I've watched waves of change come through. My father has been in technology his entire career—a Technical Program Manager III who builds things from the ground up. My mother was for a short time a volunteer EMT who had to stay calm while everything around her was in crisis. I grew up understanding, almost by osmosis, that the right response to change is not panic—it's preparation, adaptation, and a steady hand.

AI is not here to destroy us. AI is here to push us forward, to help us build faster, think bigger, and focus our human energy on the things that machines genuinely cannot do: judgment, empathy, leadership, and the kind of quiet courage it takes to keep a team moving when nothing is certain.

Those things have always mattered. They will matter even more.

• • •

Who This Book Is For

I wrote this book for two kinds of people.

The first is someone mid-career, probably inside a large organization right now, probably feeling like the bureaucracy is winning. You know your craft. You've got the certifications, the experience, the track record. And yet somehow the right things still don't get prioritized, the wrong stakeholders still have too much influence, and your roadmap still gets derailed by forces you can't fully see or control. You're not failing. You're operating without a map in terrain that nobody adequately prepared you for.

The second is someone earlier in their career, maybe a business analyst, a project coordinator, or a technical specialist, who wants to understand how to break into enterprise or government product management. You've read the textbooks and taken the courses, but you know there's a gap between what they teach and what actually happens when you walk into a room with senior federal executives and have to defend a product decision. You want to understand how this world really works before you're inside it.

This book is for both of you. It's honest about the difficulty. It doesn't pretend the bureaucracy will cooperate or that stakeholders will always be reasonable. But it is fundamentally optimistic, because I've lived this career and I genuinely believe that the skills required to lead in complex, regulated, high-stakes environments are some of the most transferable and valuable skills a professional can build, and almost nobody is talking about how to build them.

• • •

How to Use This Book

The book is organized into four parts. Part One is about understanding the environment: before you can lead effectively inside a large organization, you have to understand why it works the way it does. Part Two is the tactical playbook: roadmaps, backlogs, Agile in the real world, data, metrics, and the build-versus-buy decisions that nobody ever makes cleanly. Part Three is about leadership without a mandate: influence, coaching, executive communication, and what to do when things break. Part Four is about your career: how to grow, how to pivot, and how to position the skills you've built so that they travel.

You can read it straight through, or you can go directly to the chapters that address your most pressing challenges. Each chapter ends with a set of practical takeaways: things you can think about, try, or implement before your next sprint, your next stakeholder meeting, your next difficult conversation.

My only ask is that you bring your real situation with you. Don't read this as theory. Read it as a conversation between you and someone who has been in the room you're about to walk into—and made it through.

• • •

That first church service I directed was choppy. There were missed cues, moments of silence that stretched too long, a camera cut that happened half a beat late. But it came together. The service happened. The team made it through. And the next time I stood in front of that crew, I was a little better. And the time after that, a little better still.

That's how this work goes. You don't learn it in a weekend. You learn it by doing it, by failing a little, by finding the people who believe in you, and by refusing to let the doubters in the room write the ending of your story.

Let's get to work.

— *Nathaniel Dull*

PART ONE
Understanding the Environment

CHAPTER ONE

The Bureaucracy Is Not Your Enemy

Here is something nobody tells you early enough in this career: the bureaucracy is not broken.

I know how that sounds. I know what it feels like at 4:30 on a Friday when a compliance review has just pushed your release date back six weeks, when a policy that hasn't been updated in three years is blocking a decision that everyone in the room agrees needs to be made, when leadership has shifted priorities again and the roadmap you spent a quarter building is suddenly in question. In those moments, the system feels broken. It feels irrational. It feels like the enemy.

But it isn't. And the day you truly understand that, not just intellectually but in your bones, is the day your effectiveness as a product leader in a large organization changes permanently.

• • •

The SharePoint Gauntlet

Let me tell you about upgrading SharePoint inside a federal agency.

When I was managing the enterprise SharePoint platform at the Centers for Medicare and Medicaid Services, the system served roughly 6,000 federal civilian employees and up to 3,000 contractors simultaneously. It was the connective tissue of the agency: document management, collaboration, workflows, applications, and eventually with the shift to Microsoft 365, a platform that could do things most of our users hadn't even imagined yet.

And like any software platform, it had to be upgraded. Regularly. Microsoft's servicing timelines don't care about federal budget cycles or administration transitions, or a security authorization package still working its way through the approval process. The deadline is the deadline.

Over the years, we moved that platform through multiple major versions: from SharePoint 2009 to 2013, from 2013 to 2016, from 2016 to 2019, and eventually we made the decision to skip SE entirely and migrate directly to SharePoint Online in Microsoft 365. Each upgrade was a full-scale coordination effort across infrastructure teams, security teams, contract teams, third-party tool vendors, and a user base of nearly 9,000 people who had built their workflows and processes on top of whatever version we were currently running.

Every upgrade taught me the same lesson, over and over, in different forms: the obstacle is almost never the technology. The obstacle is the system that surrounds the technology.

Third-party tools that had worked fine in one version would suddenly announce they were discontinuing support. Competing programs within the agency would see the migration as an opportunity to advocate for moving users to their platform instead. Funding would get questioned mid-project. A new administration would bring new leadership with different priorities. Security requirements would shift. NARA compliance (National Archives records management) added its own layer of scrutiny to everything we moved or decommissioned.

And through all of it, the bureaucracy kept doing exactly what it was designed to do: slow things down, require documentation, demand justification, protect the institution from risk.

For a long time, I experienced that as friction. Eventually, I learned to experience it as information.

• • •

Why the System Works the Way It Does

Large organizations, and federal agencies especially, are not optimized for speed. They are optimized for accountability, continuity, and risk management. When you understand that, the behavior that used to feel irrational starts to make a different kind of sense.

The compliance review that pushed your release date back six weeks? It exists because at some point in the past, something went wrong without that review in place, and someone was accountable for the consequences. The policy that hasn't been updated in three years? It was written by someone who no longer works there, in response to a problem you may not know the history of, and nobody has had the bandwidth or the mandate to revisit it. The leadership pivot that disrupted your roadmap? It reflects priorities that were probably shaped by budget conversations, political pressures, or strategic decisions made at levels above what you can see.

None of this is personal. None of it is irrational on its own terms. The system is doing what systems do: protecting itself, managing competing demands, and trying to serve an enormous number of stakeholders simultaneously.

Your job is not to defeat that system. Your job is to understand it well enough to move within it effectively.

• • •

The PR Mindset That Changes Everything

I graduated from Northwestern University in St. Paul with a degree in Broadcasting/Electronic Media. For a long time, I thought of that as background noise to my technology career, interesting and formative but not directly relevant to product management inside a federal agency.

I was wrong.

The single most powerful tool I developed over my years at CMS wasn't a methodology or a framework. It was the ability to communicate the value of a product so compellingly that the people who could fund it, protect it, or kill it chose to fund and protect it instead.

SharePoint is a perfect example. Most people, even most people who use it every day, think of it as a document management system. A place to store files. Maybe a team site. SharePoint is, in their mental model, a utility: necessary, a little boring, not worth much political capital.

That mental model nearly got our program defunded more than once.

What we actually had was an enterprise application platform. We were building custom apps, designing automated workflows, managing critical business processes, and with the migration to Microsoft 365, opening up capabilities through Power Platform that would have cost millions of dollars to build from scratch on any other system. The "simple document management tool" was generating real, measurable business value—millions of dollars in cost savings, 300 automation improvements, 99.9 percent system uptime across 104 site collections and 1,300 project sites.

But value that isn't communicated isn't perceived. And value that isn't perceived doesn't get protected.

I delivered 115 executive briefings over the course of that program. Not because leadership kept forgetting what we did. But because in a large organization, the story of your product's value has to be told continuously, at every level, in language that each audience finds meaningful.

That is a communications job as much as it is a product job.

• • •

Reframing the Bureaucracy

Stop asking: "How do I get around this obstacle?"

Start asking: "What is this obstacle trying to protect, and how do I work with that?"

The compliance requirement isn't trying to block you. It's trying to protect the agency from a risk. If you can demonstrate that your approach addresses the risk, better, faster, and more completely than the existing process, the compliance requirement becomes an ally, not an obstacle.

The competing program that's advocating for your users to migrate to their platform isn't your enemy. They're your reminder that you need to be continuously demonstrating your product's value, or someone else will fill that narrative vacuum for you.

The leadership pivot that disrupted your roadmap isn't a betrayal. It's a signal about what the organization actually values right now, and your job is to find the thread that connects your work to those current priorities and pull on it.

This is not naivety. I'm not telling you to pretend the friction doesn't exist or that every institutional obstacle has a clean solution. Some of them don't. Some of them will slow you down no matter what you do, and the right response is patience and a long game, not a breakthrough.

What I'm telling you is that the orientation matters. Leaders who experience the bureaucracy as an enemy spend enormous energy fighting it. Leaders who experience it as terrain spend that same energy navigating it. The terrain leaders consistently outperform, outlast, and out-deliver the fighters. I've watched it happen again and again.

• • •

The Leadership Lifeline

One more thing from those SharePoint years that I have to name directly: I was fortunate to have good leadership behind me, and it made an enormous difference.

There were moments when the program was at risk: when defunding was a real possibility, when an administration change brought new scrutiny, when competing priorities threatened to pull resources away. In those moments, having senior leaders who understood the value of what we were building and were willing to go to bat for it was not a nice-to-have. It was the difference between the program surviving and not.

I lost good leadership at one point and gained new good leadership at another. I've experienced both sides of that equation, and I can tell you that one of the most important strategic investments you can make as a product leader is the relationship you build with the people above you. Not through politics or flattery, but through the consistent delivery of results, the proactive communication of value, and the demonstrated ability to handle problems before they become crises.

Your leadership team cannot protect what they don't understand. Your job is to make sure they always understand what you're building, why it matters, and what it would cost the organization to lose it.

• • •

The 508 Lesson I Did Not See Coming

The first major SharePoint upgrade I managed taught me something about the bureaucracy that no briefing document or onboarding session had prepared me for. I had my plan. The technical approach was solid. The timeline was realistic. What I had not thought about, not once, was Section 508.

Section 508 refers to an amendment to the Workforce Rehabilitation Act of 1973 that requires federal agencies to make their electronic and information technology accessible to people with disabilities. In practical terms, this means that any application, website, or digital tool used by federal employees must be usable by someone who is blind, deaf, or has a motor impairment. It is not a suggestion. It is a mandate with teeth.

What I did not know, walking into that first upgrade cycle, was that 508 compliance testing was not something you could satisfy by downloading a document from Microsoft. A Voluntary Product Accessibility Template (a VPAT) is a standardized form that software vendors publish to describe how their product meets accessibility standards. Microsoft provides VPATs for SharePoint. Getting that document was the easy part. The easy part was never the part that cost you.

The hard part was what came after. You had to write your own test scripts: detailed, step-by-step documentation of every action a normal user might take within the application, written as if you were explaining the system to someone who had never seen it. You had to test those workflows using a JAWS screen reader, which stands for Job Access With Speech. JAWS is a software application that translates the visual content of a screen into synthesized speech, allowing users who are blind or have significant vision impairments to navigate digital environments entirely by sound. Testing a SharePoint site with JAWS means going through every link, every button, every form field, every navigation element, and verifying that it reads correctly, in the right order, with the right labels, because a screen reader does not forgive a poorly labeled button or a form that lacks proper focus management.

The first time I sat down with the 508 compliance team, it was genuinely intimidating. Not because the people were difficult (they were not), but because the scope of what they were asking for was larger than I had anticipated. Many pages of documentation. Test scripts I would have to write myself. A full accessibility audit of the application before it could go live. And if something failed, if a user workflow did not pass the JAWS test or if a high-severity finding came back—you had two options: fix it, or get a waiver. And getting a waiver was not a casual process.

The 508 compliance team had the authority to shut down your application if critical accessibility findings were not addressed within the required timeframe. That is not a bureaucratic inconvenience. It is a legal protection for the people who depend on accessible technology to do their jobs.

I will be honest about where I started. Early in my career, I thought of 508 compliance as a checkbox, something you did because you had to and not because you understood why. The paperwork was complex. The testing was labor-intensive. The timelines it imposed on upgrade projects were real and sometimes painful. I was not hostile to it, but I was not a believer either.

That changed over years of working with the 508 team directly. CMS employs people with a wide range of disabilities. Federal agencies have stronger legal mandates and, in many cases, stronger actual practices around disability inclusion than most private sector organizations. The work the 508 team was doing was not bureaucratic obstruction. It was ensuring that a colleague who uses a screen reader could access the same systems, perform the same functions, and do the same job as everyone else. That is not a minor thing. That is the point.

By the time I had been through multiple upgrade cycles, my relationship with the 508 compliance process had changed completely. I was no longer filling out forms because I had to. I was working with the team, sometimes helping them with internal communications, sometimes collaborating on how to explain accessibility requirements to vendors who did not fully understand what was being asked of them. The compliance requirement that had once felt like a wrench thrown into my planning became something I actually believed in.

We always passed our 508 testing. I am proud of that. Not because it was easy (it was not), but because it meant that what we built actually worked for everyone who needed to use it.

The lesson I want to leave you with is the one I learned slowly, through repetition and genuine relationship: the bureaucratic requirements that feel most burdensome in the early stages of your career are often the ones protecting something worth protecting.

You do not always see it from where you are standing at the beginning. But the view changes when you understand the mission behind the mandate.

Before the Next Chapter

Three things to reflect on before you move forward:

→ Think about the obstacle in your current work that frustrates you most. What is it actually protecting? Is there a way to address that underlying concern rather than fight the obstacle directly?

→ When did someone last outside your immediate team articulate the value of what you're building—in their own words? If you can't answer that, you have a communication gap worth closing.

→ Who in your leadership chain truly understands what your product does and why it matters? If the answer is "nobody above my direct manager," that is a strategic vulnerability, and it is yours to fix.

CHAPTER TWO

Stakeholders Without a Map

Somewhere in my career I stopped being surprised by this, but it took longer than I'd like to admit.

You're deep into a project. The intake went smoothly. Discovery went well. Development is humming. You're in QA, wrapping things up, almost at the finish line, and then a new face appears on the call. Someone you've never seen before. They're introduced as the group director, or the division director, technical advisor, or simply as "so-and-so's boss." They're curious, they say. Excited to see what the team has been working on.

And then they start talking. And within ten minutes, the product you have nearly finished is no longer the product anyone is building.

The ghost stakeholder has arrived. And they've brought a completely different vision with them.

• • •

The Three Stakeholder Traps

In my years managing enterprise IT programs inside the federal government, I encountered variations of this scenario more times than I can count. Over time I came to recognize three distinct traps, each with its own flavor and its own fix.

Trap One: The Subject Matter Expert Who Doesn't Have the Full Picture

This is the most common one. A subject matter expert, someone doing the actual day-to-day work, submits a ticket or initiates a project request. They know their piece of the problem intimately. They've thought carefully about what they need. They're engaged, responsive, and genuinely trying to help.

What they often don't realize is that they're not the whole story. Their boss has opinions. Their downstream colleagues who will actually use the workflow have needs. There are people adjacent to this project, in other divisions, on other teams, who will be affected by whatever gets built and who have never been asked a single question.

The SME isn't hiding this from you. They genuinely may not know. They're focused on their lane, and your job is to look beyond it on their behalf.

The person who submits the ticket is rarely the complete picture of who the product needs to serve. Your first intake conversation should always be treated as the beginning of stakeholder discovery, not the end of it.

I redesigned my intake process more than once because of this trap. The fix, eventually, was simple: make the question standard. At every first meeting, before we talked about requirements or timelines or technical approach, I asked the same thing: "Is there anyone else who should be in this conversation? Your manager, perhaps, or colleagues who'll use whatever we build downstream?"

Sometimes the answer was no. But often enough, that question surfaced someone critical who would otherwise have shown up at the worst possible moment, usually near the finish line.

• • •

Trap Two: The Late-Arriving Boss

This is the trap that most Product Managers in large organizations have experienced at least once, and it is the most disruptive of the three.

The project is nearly done. You're in testing, or wrapping up documentation, or preparing for launch. And then a senior leader—someone several levels above the person you've been working with—decides to tune in. They arrive without context. They haven't sat through the discovery sessions or the design reviews or the iterations. They see the product fresh, through the lens of whatever they imagined it would be, which is almost certainly not what was scoped because they were never part of the scoping conversation.

And they have opinions. Strong ones. And because of their title, those opinions carry weight that immediately reshapes the room.

A product designed in a single late-stage conversation with a senior leader who wasn't part of the process is almost never a product that serves users well. It's a product that reflects what someone powerful imagined, unchecked by the reality of what users actually need.

What happens next, and what I have watched happen many times, plays out in a predictable arc. The deadline gets extended.

Sometimes by weeks, sometimes by multiple iterations, sometimes by months. The new stakeholder may struggle to make decisions because they're not fully briefed. Or they become hyperfocused on one element while the larger picture drifts. Or the project simply loses momentum as the team waits for clarity that keeps getting deferred.

I have watched projects get stretched across many additional iterations trying to satisfy a stakeholder who arrived late and whose vision kept evolving. Not because they were unreasonable people—most weren't—but because they were being asked to make consequential product decisions without the foundational context that makes those decisions grounded. They were guessing, and you were building against guesses.

The fix for this trap has two parts. The first is proactive: identify senior stakeholders early and find a way to get at least a brief touchpoint with them during discovery, even if it's a fifteen-minute conversation. Not to get approval on every decision, but to surface their assumptions before they become late-stage surprises.

The second part requires some nerve: when the late-arriving leader shows up with strong opinions, your job is not to immediately fold. It's to walk them through what was scoped, why those decisions were made, and what changing direction at this stage would actually cost. Sometimes they'll adjust. Sometimes they won't. But either way, you've done your job by making sure the decision is an informed one.

We eventually added a structural fix that helped significantly: a management sign-off requirement on the intake form. Before a project moved into development, the stakeholder's manager had to acknowledge the scope. It didn't eliminate late arrivals entirely—nothing does—but it created a paper trail that grounded those conversations. When a director showed up at QA with a new vision, we could return to the document their manager had signed and have a much more productive conversation about what had changed and why.

• • •

Trap Three: The Senior Leader Who Won't Get in the Room

This one is subtler, and in some ways the most corrosive of the three—because it doesn't announce itself the way the others do. There's no dramatic late arrival. No ghost stakeholder materializing at the finish line. Just a sustained absence at the top, and a chain of intermediaries doing their best to carry a vision they can only partially see.

The pattern is this: a senior leader initiates a project, or blesses one that has been initiated in their name, and then never engages with the work directly. Everything comes through a layer of intermediaries: a special assistant, a deputy, a well-meaning middle manager carrying their best interpretation of what the leader wants. Each of those people is trying to help. None of them is the decision-maker. And the gap between what they relay and what the leader actually envisions widens with every sprint, every review, every round of feedback that arrives secondhand and slightly off.

The result is a project that gets completed—technically—but that never quite feels right. You built what you were told to build. You just were never sure whether the person who told you was telling you the right thing. That uncertainty compounds over time, and it is expensive: in rework, in lost confidence, in the quiet erosion of the team's belief that what they are building is wanted.

Getting a senior leader in the room for thirty minutes of discovery will save you months of rework. Your job is to make that ask compellingly enough that it gets a yes.

The fix has two parts. The first is getting the leader in the room, at least once, before the work goes far. Not for every review, which is neither realistic nor necessary. But for the foundational conversation: what does success look like to you, in your own words, and what would make this not worth having built? Twenty minutes of that conversation is worth more than twenty sprints of secondhand interpretation. The way I learned to make this ask was to reframe it: not a "meeting" but a "brief alignment session"—a specific, bounded investment of their time that protects them from a much larger one later. Most senior leaders, presented that way, understood the trade-off.

The second part is building the lateral network when the official channel goes unreliable. In a large organization, there are almost always people at or near the senior leader's level who understand their priorities, have genuine access to their thinking, and are willing to engage with your work if you give them the right opening. Finding those people, not to route around leadership, but to stay oriented toward the real goal when the direct line goes quiet, is one of the more underappreciated skills in enterprise product management.

• • •

Building Your Real Stakeholder Map

Underlying all three traps is the same fundamental problem: the official org chart tells you who exists, but it doesn't tell you who matters, who influences, or who can quietly derail your work from three levels above or two cubicles over.

For every project I managed, I tried to answer four questions about each stakeholder I identified. First: what do they want from this project, and what do they fear? Second: how much influence do they actually have over the outcome, regardless of their title? Third: who do they talk to that I might not have considered? And fourth: what would it take for them to become an active advocate rather than a late-stage obstacle?

The answers to those questions don't come from org charts. They come from conversations, from observation, from the institutional knowledge of colleagues who've worked in the organization longer than you have. They come from asking, at every meeting, whether there's someone who should be in the room who isn't.

The map is never complete. But a working map, updated regularly, is infinitely better than navigating blind—which is what you're doing every time you assume the person who submitted the ticket is the whole story.

• • •

The Dashboard Nobody Could Fully Own

The dashboard project was the clearest version of this I have experienced. A senior leader wanted visibility into program performance: something that surfaced key metrics, presented them cleanly, and could be used in briefings. It was a reasonable ask. The problem was that the senior leader was never in the room.

Everything came through a special assistant, a capable person genuinely trying to help, carrying their own interpretation of what the senior leader wanted. Early on, we took that at face value. We built based on the direction we were given. We iterated. We adjusted. We showed our work. And the direction kept changing in ways that did not quite add up, changes that felt like they were coming from somewhere other than the person we were building for.

There was a meeting, and I remember it clearly, where we walked through the latest iteration and the special assistant gave us feedback that contradicted something they had explicitly approved two sprints before. The language was careful. The reasoning was thin. And what I felt in that moment was not frustration, exactly, but a kind of clarity: this feedback was not theirs. It was filtered. We were getting signals from the senior leader through a channel that was not transmitting them cleanly.

The filtered stakeholder problem is not about dishonesty. The problem is about the inevitable distortion that happens when one person translates another person's vision, especially when the vision is not fully formed to begin with.

We made a decision. Rather than continue building against secondhand interpretation, we started building the network laterally, reaching out to other directors who interacted with the senior leader, people who understood their priorities and could give us a more grounded picture of what they actually needed. In a large organization, there is almost always someone at or near the decision-maker's level who will engage directly with your work if you give them the right opening. We found that person. They were genuinely helpful. They could push things through, provide real direction, and give us feedback that felt like it came from somewhere with actual authority.

Did we ever get full certainty? No. There was a version of the dashboard we delivered that I am fairly confident landed somewhere in the vicinity of what was wanted, close enough to be accepted and used. Whether it was exactly right—whether it matched the image in the senior leader's head when they first made the request—I cannot tell you. What I can tell you is that we found a way to get directional signal when the official channel had become unreliable, and we used that signal to build something functional rather than spinning indefinitely on secondhand interpretation.

That experience changed how I approach large projects with distant senior stakeholders. I now build the lateral network deliberately, from the beginning. Not to route around leadership, but to ensure that when the official channel goes quiet or unclear, there are other informed people in the system who can help you stay oriented toward the real goal.

Before the Next Chapter

Three things to reflect on before you move forward:

→ Think about a project that went sideways due to a stakeholder who showed up late or wasn't initially included. What was the first signal you missed? What would you ask in the intake conversation now that you didn't ask then?

→ For your current most important initiative: draw out the real stakeholder map, not the org chart. Who has influence that isn't reflected in their title? Who hasn't been in a single conversation yet but could reshape the outcome if they showed up?

→ Is there a senior leader whose input you need but haven't been able to access directly? What would a reframed ask look like, one that respects their time while making clear what the cost of their absence is?

CHAPTER THREE

Compliance Is a Feature, Not a Bug

Some people I came to call the rulemakers.

They are the hardworking men and women inside agencies like CMS whose job is to look at massive, complex federal programs and figure out how to make them work better for the American people. They write the policies. They interpret the regulations. They translate the priorities of each administration into the actual rules that govern how healthcare is administered across the entire country. The work they do is consequential in ways that most people who interact with a SharePoint site on a Monday morning never stop to consider.

They also, it turns out, work around the clock. Weekends included.

I learned this the hard way.

• • •

The Announcement Nobody Reads Until It Affects Them

When you manage an enterprise platform serving thousands of users, upgrades are not optional. Software has a lifecycle. Microsoft's servicing timelines don't negotiate. At some point, the version you're running stops receiving security updates, and at that point you have a compliance problem that is far more serious than any upgrade inconvenience.

So we would plan. We would schedule. We would send announcements. And then, reliably, as the upgrade window approached, people would come out of the woodwork. Most users would shrug. A weekend offline was inconvenient but manageable.

The rulemakers were not most users. For them, the application wasn't a convenience. It was the infrastructure of their work. When we announced a weekend upgrade, they didn't shrug. They escalated.

The people who push back hardest on your timeline are almost always the people who depend on your product most. That pushback is not an obstacle. That friction is the most valuable user research you will ever receive, and it arrives for free.

We had some heated conversations in those early upgrade cycles. Timelines got moved, sometimes by weeks, sometimes longer. There were moments of real friction, the kind where you're in a meeting and the room feels like it's contracting around you and every option on the table seems to create a new problem somewhere else.

Those moments were not failures. They were the system working exactly as it should.

• • •

When Compliance Costs You Something Real

The "compliance is a feature" framing can obscure something: there were times when compliance genuinely hurt. Not in abstract or theoretical ways, but in real, operational, immediate ways that cost the program time, stakeholder goodwill, and occasionally my sleep.

The most consistent source of that pain was governance around permissions.

When I inherited the SharePoint environment at CMS, it was what I would describe as the Wild West. Nearly everyone had administrative access. People were creating sites, deleting content, building workflows, and modifying configurations without coordination or oversight. The result was an environment that was genuinely out of control: stale data everywhere, broken workflows that nobody had maintained, sites that had been abandoned but never removed, and a security posture that made our information security colleagues deeply uncomfortable.

So we did what the situation required: we built governance. We modeled permissions properly. We took away the admin access that most people should never have had in the first place and replaced it with contribute access appropriate to their actual needs. We established the structure that an enterprise platform serving 9,000 people needs to be maintained reliably and securely.

And then the calls started coming in.

In a large organization, governance feels like restriction to the people it governs. Your job is not to apologize for the structure. Your job is to help people understand what the structure protects, and to make the legitimate path as smooth as possible so the shortcuts stop looking attractive.

Senior leaders who were used to having admin access wanted to know why it had been taken away. Division directors who had been spinning up sites on a whim were frustrated that the process now required coordination. Contractors from other programs who had previously accessed our environment freely were angry that permissions now required justification.

I understood the frustration. I had been a contractor myself. I knew what it felt like to encounter a process that seemed designed to make your work harder. But I also knew, in a way that was harder to communicate across a conference call to a frustrated director, that the alternative, an environment with no governance where anyone could do anything—wasn't actually serving anyone well. It just wasn't causing visible pain yet.

Part of the challenge is a genuine knowledge gap. When someone demands admin access, they often don't know what admin access actually means. They assume it means "full access to do my job" when it actually means "full access to delete, modify, or break anything in the environment, including things that don't belong to you." They need edit access. They've asked for admin access because those two things sound similar to them, and nobody has explained the difference.

We learned to lean into that education rather than just enforcing the rule. When a stakeholder was upset about a permissions decision, the most effective response was not a policy citation. It was a conversation: here is what you're actually trying to do, here is the access level that enables that, and here is why giving you more than that creates risks you probably don't want to own. Most reasonable people, when they understood the real picture, got there. Not immediately, and not always cheerfully. But they got there.

The governance held. The Wild West did not return. And over time, as the platform stabilized and the benefits of a well-maintained environment became visible, even the most resistant stakeholders stopped fighting the structure. Some of them became its defenders—because they had watched what happened when a peer's unmanaged site caused a problem that affected their work, and they understood viscerally what governance was protecting.

• • •

What Compliance Actually Protects

Federal agencies operate within fiscal years that end in September and begin in October. Administration transitions bring new priorities. Policy windows open and close. The rulemakers at CMS weren't being difficult when they told us our September upgrade window didn't work for them. They were telling us something true and important about the nature of their work.

What we eventually understood was that compliance constraints and regulatory rhythms weren't arbitrary. They reflected the actual operating reality of the people we served. Once we internalized that, our approach to planning changed fundamentally. We stopped treating compliance constraints as obstacles to work around and started treating them as requirements to design for.

• • •

Turning Critics Into Champions

After those early heated conversations, we made a deliberate decision. The stakeholders who had pushed back hardest would become the first people we called when we came back online. We backed up their data. We tested with them first. We sat with them and walked through every change, making sure nothing had been lost.

They became our most vocal advocates.

The user who makes your life hardest is often the user who cares most about your product. Find a way to serve them well, and you've found your most powerful advocates.

This dynamic played out beyond the upgrade cycles too. Because we had built those relationships, stakeholders would come to us with other problems: legacy processes nobody had looked at in years, workflows quietly causing pain. Problems we never would have known about if we hadn't earned the trust that made people comfortable bringing them to us.

• • •

The Communication Lesson You Can't Skip

One of the most consistent mistakes I've seen Product Managers make in large, regulated environments is treating communication as a final step. By that point, you've already lost the opportunity to surface the constraints that would have changed your plan.

We learned to communicate early and broadly, even when we didn't have everything figured out. A well-timed, honest communication—"We're planning an upgrade in this window, and we want to know if that creates problems for anyone"—is one of the most powerful discovery tools available. It costs almost nothing. The information it returns can be worth months of rework avoided.

After every major upgrade, every significant project, we did a lessons learned review. Those reviews weren't a formality. They were where the institutional knowledge lived: the accumulated wisdom of what this particular environment required, built up one project at a time. If you aren't doing lessons learned in your organization, you are paying for the same education over and over again.

• • •

The Moment You Wonder If It Is Worth It

There were moments when I genuinely wondered if holding the governance line was worth the political cost. Not abstractly. Specifically.

When you have senior leaders calling your management and your management looks at you and says "are you sure you want to do this?"—that is a real moment. That is a moment where the easier path is right in front of you, clearly marked, and nobody in the room would think less of you for taking it. Give them what they're asking for. Move on. Stop having this fight.

What kept me from folding was not stubbornness, and it was not policy. It was a specific mental image: the Wild West we had inherited. An environment where anyone could grant themselves administrative access, where people did exactly that, where data was stale and broken workflows were scattered across the platform like debris from a hundred small decisions that nobody had ever cleaned up. We had built something out of that. We had created structure. And I knew, with genuine certainty, that if we opened the door on permissions, the Wild West would return. Not eventually. Quickly.

The temptation to give in on governance is highest exactly when governance is doing its job. The friction is not a sign that the structure is wrong. That resistance is a sign that the structure is real.

There was also something I noticed about the nature of the requests. People were not asking for contribute access so they could do their jobs. They were asking for admin access because admin access is how they had always done it. Giving them contribute access, the appropriate level that actually matched their needs, was not actually a problem for their work. It felt like a problem because it was different. And different in a large organization generates friction automatically, regardless of whether the change is an improvement.

Other systems around us had stronger governance than we did. Teams would come to us with requirements that our own governance structure actually satisfied, and they would push back anyway, not because our approach was wrong but because they were used to getting exceptions elsewhere. A specific bureaucratic dynamic emerges where governance becomes uneven across an organization, and that unevenness creates its own frustrations. Why do I have to follow the rules when the other team doesn't? That is a fair question. The answer—that we were not responsible for how other teams ran their systems, only for how we ran ours—was true but not always satisfying.

I kept going because I knew what the alternative looked like. I had seen it. We had cleaned it up once. Doing it again was not a project I wanted to manage. And over time, as the platform stabilized and the benefits became visible, the same people who had been most resistant became the ones most willing to defend the structure when something went wrong in someone else's environment. They had experienced what good governance produced. That experience turned them.

• • •

They never acknowledged it afterward. That was fine. Acknowledgment was not what I was looking for. What I was looking for was a platform that would still be functional and auditable two years later, and that is what we got.

The argument we made was a simple one: if we gave exceptions when pressured, we would get more pressure. If it became known that the way to get around the permission structure was to escalate to senior leadership, every request would eventually become an escalation. Other systems across the agency held hard governance lines. There was no logical reason ours should be softer. We had already paid the price of cleaning up what happens when governance is soft. We were not going to pay it twice.

So we held. Not combatively, not dismissively, but firmly. My director was clear that the decision was ours to make and that leadership would be informed of the reasoning. That backing mattered. Holding a governance line is genuinely difficult when senior stakeholders are expressing frustration above you, and having a director who said, in effect, if you want to fight this I'll be there alongside you, made it possible to stand on the principle without it feeling like a personal standoff.

The contractors were a different problem. Giving contractors administrator rights in an enterprise platform is a governance risk that compounds over time. Contractors rotate. Contracts end. When someone with administrator access leaves a project, that access does not automatically disappear. It has to be tracked, audited, and removed manually, and in a large environment with dozens of contractors across multiple vendors, that tracking is exactly the kind of thing that gets missed. We had seen the downstream effects of exactly that problem in the environment we inherited. We were not going to recreate it.

When the directors came asking for administrator access, they were not asking in bad faith. Most of them did not fully understand what administrator access meant or what they actually needed to accomplish what they were trying to do. What they needed was site owner access, or in many cases simply contributor rights: enough to do their work, no more. The gap between what they were asking for and what they actually needed was not technical. It was a communication gap, and part of my job was to close it.

Cleaning it up the first time was one of the harder projects of my career. And the governance structure we put in place after that cleanup was specifically designed to prevent the same thing from happening again. Three or four permission levels, defined clearly, applied consistently. No custom permission configurations, because every custom configuration is a future migration problem waiting to happen. Site creation controlled and tracked. Ownership documented.

This is what ungoverned looks like in practice. Not dramatic failure. Just accumulated entropy: thousands of small decisions made without coordination, each one individually harmless, collectively producing a system that no one could fully understand, audit, or trust.

The sites themselves were just as chaotic. Everyone had their own piece of the environment and they treated it accordingly. There were sites filled with personal documents. There were sites with photos from office parties, retirement celebrations, informal collections of things that had no business living in an enterprise platform. There were test sites created by developers experimenting with something years ago, now abandoned, the people who built them long gone, nobody aware the sites even existed. There were sites that had not been accessed in so long that the ownership trail was completely cold.

The Wild West I inherited was not a metaphor. It was a documentation problem, a security problem, a maintenance problem, and a user experience problem all layered on top of each other in a way that made each one harder to solve. When I took over the SharePoint environment, what I found was a sprawl that had grown without coordination for years. A single site collection, which in a well-governed environment might contain three or four permission groups, clearly named and clearly scoped, would sometimes contain twenty, thirty, fifty different groups. The same people would appear in six of them, holding identical access through different paths. Some of those groups had thousands of members. Some of those members had not touched the system in years. Nobody had cleaned it up because nobody had owned it.

Before the Next Chapter

Three things to reflect on before you move forward:

→ Who are the rulemakers in your organization—the people whose compliance needs or operational rhythms most constrain your planning? Do you know them by name? Have you had a real conversation with them about how your product affects their work?

→ Think about the last time a compliance requirement or governance decision made a stakeholder angry. Did you explain what the structure was protecting, or did you default to policy citation? What would the educational version of that conversation have looked like?

→ When was the last time you did a genuine lessons learned review? If it's been a while, that's probably the answer. The education is already paid for. You might as well collect it.

PART TWO
The Craft of Enterprise Product Leadership

CHAPTER FOUR

Roadmaps Nobody Ignores

A roadmap that lives only in a slide deck is not a roadmap. That document is a wish list with better formatting.

I have seen plenty of both. The difference between them is not the quality of the planning or the clarity of the vision, although those things matter. The difference is whether the roadmap is built to survive contact with the real environment: the budget cycles, the administration transitions, the competing priorities, the technical discoveries that rewrite your assumptions halfway through execution.

In a large organization, a roadmap that can't survive those forces won't. And a roadmap that nobody believes in won't be protected when those forces arrive. Building a roadmap that holds up, one that people fight for rather than quietly abandon when things get hard, is one of the most important skills in enterprise product management. Metrics are also among the least talked about.

Let me tell you about three roadmaps. One that held. One that changed course and delivered faster because of it. And one that got overruled by leadership, sat with the consequences, and eventually was proven right.

• • •

The SharePoint 2019 Migration: Building the Roadmap on Evidence

Of all the platform upgrades I managed at CMS, the migration to SharePoint 2019 was the most technically complex. The framework had changed fundamentally from previous versions. Things that worked in SharePoint 2016 did not simply carry forward. Workflows behaved differently. The architecture was different. Even our team had mixed information about what the upgrade would actually require in practice.

In that environment, high complexity and high stakes with incomplete information, the instinct is often to plan anyway. To take your best estimate, build a roadmap around it, and commit to a timeline that projects confidence even when the underlying confidence isn't fully earned.

We didn't do that. Instead, we ran a proof of concept.

The POC lasted somewhere between three months and six months. It was not a small investment. But it returned something that no amount of planning in a conference room could have produced: real, specific, tested knowledge of what this upgrade would actually require. We learned which reports would break and which would survive. We learned what data had to be cleaned before migration and what could transfer cleanly. We learned what third-party tools were no longer viable and what the decommissioning process would look like. We learned where the new environment differed from our assumptions and where it matched them.

A proof of concept is not a delay to your roadmap. That proof of concept is the foundation your roadmap is built on. The teams that skip it are not moving faster. They are borrowing time they will repay at a much higher interest rate later.

By the time we built the actual migration roadmap, it was not a guess. It was a plan grounded in evidence. We knew what we were doing because we had already done a version of it. And that knowledge let us do something unusual: we split the team strategically across four parallel workstreams. Infrastructure handled the backend and the new Microsoft security requirements. A second team stood up the new environment from the ground up. Two additional teams kept existing upgrade packages and new customer work moving forward without interruption.

That last decision, to keep all other work moving while the migration happened, was a deliberate commitment we made as a team. We knew that if we paused business-as-usual work during the migration, we would lose momentum, lose users to competing platforms, and signal to leadership that our program couldn't handle complexity at scale. The report work alone was substantial: SharePoint 2019 dropped the integrated reporting mode that SharePoint 2016 had relied on entirely, which meant our existing reports couldn't simply carry forward. We were running two workstreams concurrently: converting our existing customers' reports from SharePoint integrated mode into the native mode format that 2019 required, and rebuilding from scratch the reports that couldn't be converted cleanly. Neither workstream stopped for the other. The actual cutover happened over a single weekend. Stopping that forward motion would have been costly in ways that didn't show up on a project timeline but that everyone would have felt.

The migration completed ahead of schedule. Several months earlier than planned. Everything went cleanly. The program received formal recognition for the effort, which remains one of the professional accomplishments I am most proud of. The evidence-based roadmap, the parallel workstreams, the commitment to keeping forward motion on all fronts: it all held together because the foundation was real.

• • •

The New Job Pivot: When the Roadmap Has to Change on Day One

Not every roadmap story is about building something that holds. Sometimes the most important thing a product leader can do is recognize, quickly and clearly, that the existing plan is wrong, and say so out loud before the organization invests further in the wrong direction.

I joined a new organization and was hired to do a specific thing: manage the migration of an application from one platform to another. The plan was already in motion. The timeline was set. The expectation was that I would execute.

By day one, I knew the plan wasn't going to work.

I won't say the details were obvious to everyone—they weren't, or the plan wouldn't have been in place when I arrived. But from where I was standing, having come in fresh without the sunk cost of months of prior planning, the problems were visible in a way they might not have been to people who had been living inside the plan. The platform we were migrating to was not the right fit. The approach was going to create more problems than it solved.

Taking that assessment to leadership on day one of a new job is not a comfortable thing to do. You don't have credibility yet. You don't have relationships. You don't have the track record that earns you the benefit of the doubt when you walk into a room and tell people that everything they've been planning is wrong.

I did it anyway.

The most expensive words in a large organization are 'we've already come this far.' Sunk cost is not a reason to continue in the wrong direction. A failed roadmap is a reason to make sure the next decision is the right one.

Leadership listened. We changed course entirely—abandoned the original platform, redesigned the approach, and rebuilt the roadmap around a solution that actually fit the problem. What had been projected as a year-long transition compressed to six or seven months. The cost savings from that single course correction were significant. The roadmap that replaced the original one held because it was built on an honest assessment of the situation rather than momentum from prior decisions.

The lesson here is not that you should walk into every new situation and immediately challenge everything. The lesson is that a fresh perspective has genuine value, and that the willingness to surface an honest assessment, even when it is uncomfortable and even when it disrupts plans that people have emotional investment in, is one of the most important things a product leader can bring to an organization. The roadmap that changes course at the right moment is not a failed roadmap. A changed roadmap is doing exactly what roadmaps are supposed to do: reflecting reality.

• • •

The AWS Decision: When the Roadmap Gets Overruled

This is the story I almost didn't include in this chapter, because it doesn't have a clean ending where the Product Manager wins. But I think it's the most important one, because it reflects something that every practitioner in a large organization will eventually face: sometimes you build the case correctly, present the evidence clearly, and leadership still makes the call you told them not to make.

We were planning a cloud migration. Our team had done the research, deep and thoroughly documented, and our assessment was clear: the right platform for this workload was Microsoft Azure for Government. The security requirements, the integration considerations, the long-term supportability of what we were building all pointed in the same direction.

Leadership directed us to use Amazon Web Services instead.

We didn't just push back verbally. We wrote a formal paper laying out the case: the technical considerations, the risk factors, the reasons we believed AWS was the wrong choice for this specific environment and this specific workload. We presented it. We answered questions. We made the strongest case we could make with the evidence we had.

Leadership heard us. And then they told us to proceed with AWS.

So we did. You execute the decision that's been made, even when it isn't the one you recommended. That's part of the job. The roadmap absorbed the leadership decision and we moved forward.

Document your recommendations. Not to protect yourself, and not to say 'I told you so' later—but because a clear record of what was known, when it was known, and what was recommended is how organizations learn. If your recommendation was right, that record is how the next decision gets made better.

The platform proved unstable for what we were trying to do. It took time, as these things always do, but eventually the technical reality that our research had predicted became undeniable. And when it did, the migration to Microsoft Azure for Government proceeded. A second major transition, another detailed technical plan, another round of coordination with infrastructure teams and leadership and security stakeholders.

A few things are worth taking from this story. The first is that being right is not the same as winning, and in a large organization, winning is not always the point. Your job is to give leadership the best possible information, make your recommendations clearly, and then support whatever decision is made with the same professionalism you would bring to a decision you agreed with.

The second is that the paper we wrote mattered, even though it didn't change the immediate outcome. When the time came to revisit the platform decision, the case had already been made. The evidence was documented. The path forward was not a debate. It was a return to a recommendation that had already been fully developed. That saved time, and it preserved credibility, because we had never claimed to be certain about things we weren't certain about. We had simply done the work and told the truth about what we found.

The third thing is this: a roadmap that gets overruled is not a roadmap that failed. A changed plan is a roadmap that did its job: it put the right information in front of the people who needed to make the decision. What they do with that information is theirs to own. What you do with the outcome is yours.

• • •

What Makes a Roadmap Hold

Across all three of these stories, the roadmaps that held, or that changed course intelligently, had a few things in common.

They were grounded in evidence, not assumption. Whether that evidence came from a year-long POC, a day-one assessment of a new environment, or months of technical research on cloud platforms, the roadmap reflected what was known rather than what was hoped. In a large organization, the gap between assumption and evidence is where most roadmaps fail.

They were built to absorb change. The SharePoint 2019 migration ran four parallel workstreams specifically so that disruption in one area wouldn't cascade into all the others. The new job pivot succeeded partly because we hadn't over-committed to the original plan before the assessment was complete. A roadmap in a large organization has to have structural flexibility built in, not added as an afterthought when things go wrong.

They were communicated continuously. Not just at the beginning, when the plan is exciting, and not just at the end when the results are in, but throughout, at every stage, to every stakeholder who needed to understand where things stood and why. A roadmap that leadership doesn't understand cannot be protected by leadership. A roadmap that users don't believe in will not have advocates when it needs them.

And they were honest. The AWS paper was honest about the risks. The day-one pivot was honest about the problems in the existing plan. The POC was honest about what we didn't know before we started it. In a large organization, where the pressure to project confidence and certainty is constant, the product leaders who build lasting credibility are almost always the ones who tell the truth about what they know and what they don't.

That is, ultimately, what makes a roadmap nobody ignores. Not polish. Not confidence. Not the right slide template. Honesty, evidence, and the willingness to say clearly what you see, and then do the work to back it up.

• • •

Before the Next Chapter

Three things to reflect on before you move forward:

→ Look at your current roadmap. How much of it is grounded in tested evidence versus reasonable assumption? Where are the assumptions that most need to be validated before you commit further resources to them?

→ Think about a plan you've been part of that was clearly headed in the wrong direction. What stopped someone from saying so earlier? What would it have taken for that conversation to happen sooner, and what was the cost of the delay?

→ Have you ever been overruled on a recommendation you believed in? Did you document your case before the decision was made? If not, for the next one, document it. Not defensively, but so that the organization can learn from whatever happens next.

CHAPTER FIVE

Backlogs That Tell the Truth

A backlog is supposed to be a single, honest source of truth about what a team is building, in what order, and why. In practice, it is often something else entirely.

I have seen backlogs that were graveyards: hundreds of items piled in over months or years, many of them duplicates, some of them contradictory, none of them prioritized in any meaningful way. I have seen backlogs so thin they were practically empty, not because there was nothing to build but because the team was afraid to write anything down. I have seen backlogs that looked clean on the surface and were chaos underneath, full of stories so vague that two developers reading the same item would build two completely different things.

All of these backlogs have one thing in common: they are lying. And when a backlog lies, everything built on top of it is built on a foundation that will eventually give way.

• • •

The First PI Planning Disaster

I remember the first time we ran a SAFe PI Planning event at my agency. I will be honest with you: it was a disaster.

Not a catastrophic disaster. Nobody got fired. No critical systems went down. But as a planning event, as an exercise in aligning a program around shared objectives, clear dependencies, and realistic commitments—it failed. And I want to be specific about how, because the details matter.

The backlog going into that event was whatever it was, which is to say: nobody really knew. Items had been entered by different people at different times with different levels of clarity. Some of them reflected real, current priorities. Some reflected things someone had thought were important six months ago and never revisited. Some were so vague that a developer reading them would have no idea what "done" looked like. No shared definition existed, no consistent format, no clear ownership over what belonged in the backlog and what didn't.

Not everyone who should have been at the event was there. The people who were there had varying levels of familiarity with the SAFe framework: some had done reading, some had done nothing, some were encountering the concepts for the first time in the room. So when the facilitation asked for team objectives and program increment commitments, people were working without a shared mental model of what those things were supposed to look like or how they were supposed to connect.

The confusion was genuine. This wasn't people being resistant or lazy. They had been asked to work in a methodology that was new to all of them, with a backlog that hadn't been prepared for the exercise, without the shared vocabulary that makes the exercise work. The result was objectives that weren't grounded in reality, commitments that were made based on gut feel rather than actual capacity, and a general sense at the end of the event that something hadn't quite happened the way it was supposed to.

The first time a team runs a real Agile or SAFe event, it will almost certainly be messy. That messiness is not failure. It is the price of admission to a practice that takes time to develop. The teams that improve fastest are the ones who examine the mess honestly rather than pretending it didn't happen.

When it was over, we gathered the team and talked through what had happened. Not a blame session, but a genuine collective examination of what we had tried, what hadn't worked, and what we needed to understand before we tried again. We did a proper lessons learned. We identified the specific gaps: the backlog needed work, the team needed shared training, the event needed a cleaner pre-work process.

Thirteen iterations later, we had a solid, functional PI Planning process. The backlog was clean. The objectives were grounded. The team arrived prepared and left with commitments they actually believed in. That journey from the first disaster to that point was not a straight line, and it was not fast. But it started with being honest about what had gone wrong, which is the only way any of this gets better.

• • •

The Two Backlog Failure Modes

Failure Mode One: Everything Under the Sun

The first failure mode is the overloaded backlog—a dumping ground where everything lands because there is no clear ownership and prioritization discipline. People add things because they can. Customers put in requests that are really just questions. Developers add technical debt items with no business context. Business owners add features that sounded good in a meeting but haven't been validated.

Over time the backlog becomes so large and so undifferentiated that it loses its function entirely. I have sat in PI Planning sessions where the backlog had items in it that were months or years old, items referencing systems that no longer existed, items that two different people had entered independently. In those sessions the planning becomes archaeology rather than forward-looking work.

A backlog is not a parking lot. Every item in it carries a cost: the cognitive cost of evaluating it, explaining it, and deciding what to do with it every single sprint. If you wouldn't put it in the next three sprints, ask seriously whether it belongs in the backlog at all.

Failure Mode Two: The Empty Backlog

The second failure mode is the nearly empty backlog—not because there is nothing to build, but because the team is afraid to commit to anything on paper. I have seen this most often with developers who have been burned by previous environments where a story in the backlog was treated as a promise, and a promise not met was treated as a failure with consequences.

This is a learned survival behavior, and it is the direct product of a culture that conflated estimation with guarantee. When I encountered this pattern, the answer was never pressure. It was a direct, honest conversation, one on one and not in a group setting: I need you to tell me what you actually think is realistic, not what you think is safe to say. A story that doesn't complete in a sprint is information. What I can't work with is a backlog so empty we have no idea what we're building.

Most of the time, that conversation changed things. People who have been conditioned to protect themselves with ambiguity will move toward clarity when the environment genuinely rewards honesty over the appearance of certainty.

• • •

Rebuilding a Backlog That Tells the Truth

When a backlog is broken—in either direction—the fix is the same: sit down with the Scrum Master and the developer and go through it together, item by item, from the ground up. This is not a meeting you schedule for an hour and check off. Backlog refinement is a working session, sometimes several of them, asking a specific set of questions about every item: Does this still reflect a real need? Is it written clearly enough? Does it belong in this sprint, this PI, or further out?

The goal is not to have a large backlog or a small one. The goal is to have a true one.

• • •

The Cadence That Keeps It Honest

A backlog that gets cleaned up once and then neglected will deteriorate. My approach was to calibrate the cadence to the current state of the backlog. A healthy backlog might need refinement every two weeks. A backlog that had gotten out of control needed attention far more frequently, sometimes weekly or more, until it reached a state where the standard cadence could maintain it. You meet as often as the backlog requires, not as often as the calendar suggests.

The teams I have seen do this best are the ones that treat backlog health as a shared responsibility rather than a single person's job. They talk about it openly in retrospectives. They have developed a collective sense of what a healthy backlog looks like, and a shared discomfort when it starts to drift. That collective ownership doesn't come from a process document. It comes from a culture of honesty, built one conversation at a time.

• • •

What a Broken Story Actually Looks Like

Here is what the problem looks like in practice. There are projects where the "backlog" is really just the notes from the last meeting—things the developer remembers, things that came up in conversation, things that felt important in the room and then became the implicit work queue. No user stories. No acceptance criteria. No clear definition of done. Just motion in the general direction of what the customer seemed to want.

This is not laziness. This pattern develops when people have not fully internalized what backlog refinement is for. A backlog is not a memory aid for the last conversation. A sprint is a structured plan for a defined body of work: something that lets you see the whole picture before you build any single piece of it.

When you build from meeting notes instead of a backlog, you are building one piece at a time without ever seeing the full shape of what you are making. That is how you end up with a button on the wrong page.

At CMS, most of our projects had a defined beginning and end. A customer would submit a ticket, we would scope and execute the work, and when it was done, it was done. If they wanted something additional, they submitted a new ticket and we started over. That meant that for every project, even a relatively small one, there was a complete body of work that could and should be mapped out before a single line of code was written.

When I sat down with a developer and a Scrum Master to rebuild a broken backlog, we started from the intake form, what the customer had actually asked for in their own words—and worked forward from there. Not just the explicit asks, but the things you know will be required because they are always required. Does this application need a new page? Then there are permissions associated with that page. Does it have a new UI? Then there is probably a graphic design component that needs to happen before development can begin. Are there lists and libraries? Are there workflows? Are there navigation changes that will affect other parts of the system? The customer rarely comes in with a complete picture of all of that, because customers think about their problem holistically and tend to describe the thing they can see, the new button or the updated dashboard, without necessarily thinking through all the dependencies underneath it.

That is exactly why you build the backlog before you build the product. Because when you have the full picture in front of you, you realize the button should not go on this page at all. It belongs somewhere else, in a place that makes the whole system more coherent. You cannot see that when you are building one piece at a time from meeting notes. You can only see it when you have laid out the whole map.

The backlog we built from those sessions was not exhaustive on day one. You do not know everything at the start. But it was enough to plan from, enough to sequence properly, and enough to show the customer what they were getting, all of it, before they had to approve anything. That visibility, by itself, changed the nature of the conversation. Customers who could see the whole plan asked better questions and made better decisions than customers who were experiencing the product one piece at a time.

Before the Next Chapter

Three things to reflect on before you move forward:

→ Look at your current backlog with fresh eyes. Is it too full, too empty, or somewhere in between? What would it look like if every item in it was genuinely ready to be built? How many items would survive that standard?

→ Think about your developers' relationship to commitment. Are they writing stories with real specificity, or keeping things deliberately vague? If it's the latter, what conversation needs to happen—and have you created an environment where having it honestly is safe?

→ Think about whether your team has a genuine culture of commitment or a culture of vague agreement. Do estimates reflect what people actually believe they can deliver, or have they learned to hedge? If it is the latter, what in your environment created that, and what would have to change before honest commitment felt safe?

CHAPTER SIX

Agile in the Real World

Here is something about Agile that everyone says but fewer people practice: it is a framework, not a formula. The distinction is universal: you will find it in the Agile Manifesto, in the Scrum Guide, in every SAFe training course ever delivered. Nobody disputes it in the classroom. And yet in organization after organization, smart, well-credentialed practitioners arrive and apply their framework like a formula, expecting the exact model they learned in one context to produce the same results in a completely different one. Knowing something is a framework and actually treating it like one are two very different things.

A formula gives you inputs and returns a predictable output. A framework gives you structure: principles, practices, and roles designed to be adapted to the reality of the organization you are working in. The frame goes up the same way on every house. What goes inside, and what color you paint the walls, is entirely up to you.

Agile practitioners who understand this thrive in large organizations. Practitioners who don't—who arrive carrying the exact model they learned in a course and expect it to work the same way in a new context, struggle and often make the people around them struggle too.

• • •

What the Training Gets Right

Training courses are genuinely valuable. I hold SAFe and Scrum certifications, and I believe in the foundational knowledge they convey. The vocabulary, the ceremonies, the roles, the underlying principles of iterative delivery and continuous feedback, all of it matters and all of it is worth learning properly before you try to adapt it.

You cannot thoughtfully adapt a framework you don't genuinely understand. The certification is not the destination. It is the starting point for the real education, which happens on the job.

But be honest about the gap between what you learned and what you walked into. Because that gap is almost always there.

• • •

Every Organization Paints Its Walls a Different Color

In an ideal Agile world, every Scrum team has a dedicated Product Owner, a dedicated Scrum Master, and a development team of the right size. In the real world, you often find a Product Owner who is also the primary customer contact, also the business owner, also responsible for writing every requirement and attending every stakeholder meeting. You find a Scrum Master also carrying a development workload. You find a Product Manager who functions more as a program administrator because that is what the budget allows.

And in some organizations, Product Ownership has been handed entirely to a contractor, which means the person making decisions about what gets built has no organizational skin in the game and may be optimizing for contract deliverables rather than actual product outcomes.

The textbook Agile team is a useful model. The actual team you have is the one you work with. Your job is to apply the principles of the framework to the reality of your situation, not to wish the situation were different.

• • •

Where Agile Genuinely Struggles

Agile is excellent for software operations and maintenance: enhancements, iterations, incremental improvements to something that already exists. Where it struggles is in the early construction phase, when certain things simply have to happen in a specific sequence before others can begin.

You cannot build a user interface before there is a data model behind it. You cannot build a front-end React application before the API it will consume exists. You cannot spin up a new SharePoint site collection before your infrastructure team has provisioned it, and you cannot ask infrastructure to provision it before you have answered the foundational governance questions about what kind of site it should be and who should own it. These are sequential dependencies, and no amount of Agile philosophy eliminates them.

What I found in practice was that new system builds often required a hybrid approach: a structured, sequential phase to stand up the foundation, followed by an iterative phase once the foundation was stable enough to support sprint-based development on top of it. The Agile purist would call this waterfall contamination. The pragmatic product leader would call it accurate.

The same logic applies to continuous improvement and continuous development time, the investment in learning, experimentation, and innovation that SAFe and other frameworks build into the process. Many organizations refuse to invest in this time. They want to keep cranking product. They don't want to spend two weeks on something that doesn't directly ship a feature.

This is, in my experience, a costly false economy. The people on your team who have been working on the same application for years—sometimes longer than you've been in the role—are sitting on a wealth of institutional knowledge and unexplored ideas. If you never give them the space to think, to experiment, to try something they've always wondered about, you are leaving that value on the table. Worse, you are telling them implicitly that their growth doesn't matter to you. And people who feel that way start looking for organizations that feel differently.

Skipping continuous improvement doesn't save time. It borrows time from the future—from the innovation you won't have, the person you'll lose, and the technical debt you'll accumulate while everyone was too busy shipping to think.

• • •

The Story Points Conversation

Let me give you a specific example of how cultural context shapes Agile practice. Story points: if you have worked on more than one Agile team, you have had this conversation.

Story points are always related to effort—to complexity, risk, and the time a piece of work will take. The disagreement is about the scale. In some organizations, one point equals roughly one day of work. In others, one point equals one hour, or one sprint's worth of a single developer's capacity. In still others the tool doesn't support story points as the methodology intends, so teams have built workarounds that have become de facto practice long after the original reason for the workaround ceased to exist. The friction isn't about whether points are time. They are. The friction is about which unit of time, which definition of effort, and whose cultural defaults are sitting behind the number.

I have been in rooms where two experienced Agile practitioners had a heated disagreement about story points that was really a disagreement about which organization's culture each person was importing. Neither was wrong in the abstract. The right response is not to argue about which interpretation is correct. The fix is to have an explicit conversation about what convention this team will use, document it, and revisit it in a retrospective after a few sprints.

When Agile practitioners disagree about process, the disagreement is almost never about the framework. It is about which organization's adaptation of the framework each person learned from. Making that explicit is usually enough to move the conversation forward.

• • •

Transparency and the Fear of Commitment

Developers—especially contractors, especially people who have worked across multiple clients—often carry a deep wariness about committing to specific timelines. They have been in environments where an estimate became a guarantee, where missing a deadline became a performance issue, where honesty about a blocker was treated as an admission of failure. They learned, rationally, to protect themselves with vagueness.

This is not a character flaw. Fear of commitment is a rational response to bad management culture, and it will not be solved by demanding more specific commitments. It will only be solved by building an environment where people experience that honesty is safe, where a missed sprint goal becomes a conversation about what we learned, not a disciplinary note in someone's file.

That environment takes time to build. Trust is built sprint by sprint, retrospective by retrospective, through the consistent behavior of leadership that treats transparency as a gift rather than a liability. Once it exists, the commitments get more honest, the backlog gets truer, and the team gets progressively better at building what they said they would build.

• • •

Making Agile Work Where You Are

Start with the principles rather than the practices. The practices are implementations of underlying principles. Those principles are what you protect: iterative delivery, continuous feedback, working software over comprehensive documentation, responding to change over following a plan.

If your ceremonies are serving those principles, keep them. If they are not, if your sprint review has become a status report nobody learns from, if your retrospective has become a checkbox exercise, those are symptoms worth diagnosing honestly.

And if you are walking into an organization that thinks it is doing Agile but isn't—that has adopted the vocabulary without the mindset—your job is not to immediately correct everyone. The goal is to understand what they are doing, why they are doing it, and what the real framework would solve for them that their current approach is not solving. Lead from there.

The frame is the same for every house. The walls inside are yours to design. Know the difference, and you will never be confused about which one to fight for.

• • •

When the Foundation Has to Come First

The clearest example I have lived of Agile's sequential dependency problem is the project I am working on right now.

When I joined a pharmacy benefits management company and we made the decision to pivot from Power Apps to a containerized architecture on Google Cloud Platform and Google Kubernetes Engine, the first thing that became obvious was this: there was nothing to iterate on yet. The environment did not exist. The data was not connected. The team did not have access to the systems they needed to build anything. Before a single user story could be meaningfully written, a meaningful amount of work had to happen in a specific sequence, and none of it was iterative.

The foundation phase started with access. Getting the development team into GitHub, into GCP, establishing the right permissions and the right project structure. That sounds simple. In an enterprise healthcare environment with compliance requirements and security review gates, it is not simple. The work is a series of sequential dependencies: you cannot stand up the environment until the access is provisioned, you cannot provision the access until the security review is complete, you cannot complete the security review until the architecture is documented. Each step required the previous one.

While the infrastructure side was being established, we were simultaneously working to find and connect the data, identifying where it lived in GCP, understanding the table structures, standing up the data layer in a way that the application would eventually be able to query. This was not sprint work. There was no backlog for it. It was foundational architecture work that had to be resolved before there was anything for a development team to build on top of.

Then we brought in the UX designer.

You cannot design a front end for an application that does not have a defined data model behind it. The mockups tell you what the UI will look like. The data model tells you what the UI can actually do. Both have to exist before the sprint work begins, and they have to exist in the right order.

The UX designer worked from what we had established on the back end: the data structures, the known user workflows, the clinical application requirements—and began producing mockups for the front end. That design work ran alongside the continuing infrastructure and data work. It was parallel, but it was still sequential in the sense that the mockups were informing a front end that could not be built yet, because the back end it would connect to was not finished.

The moment things changed—the moment Agile actually started—was when we had enough of both sides to begin connecting them. Front end and back end stories went into Jira. We started running actual sprints: front end stories building out the React components, back end stories building out the API layer, both moving forward in parallel iterations. The back end team was working on service-to-service communication, on authentication, on the framework that would hold everything together. The front end team was building against that framework, testing connections as they matured.

From there we stood up environments in sequence: development, then staging, then production. Each environment required the data to be seeded correctly, the APIs to be connected and verified, the authentication to be working end to end before the next environment could be stood up. This is the part of a cloud-native build that looks like it should be automatable and continuous but in practice requires deliberate gates, because promoting broken code through environments creates problems that are much harder to unwind than they were to prevent.

The whole arc—from the moment the pivot decision was made to the moment we had a functioning application moving through real environments, looked almost nothing like a textbook Agile project. The first phase was sequential, structured, and not sprint-based at all. The second phase was genuinely iterative. You could not have run the second phase first. The foundation was not optional.

Agile is not an excuse to skip the foundation. Agile is a way to build effectively once the foundation exists. The teams that try to sprint before the ground is solid are not moving faster. They are building on sand, and they will find out when the tide comes in.

What I want practitioners to take from this is not that Agile is wrong for new system builds. The lesson is that the framework has to be honest about what phase of the work you are in. The foundation work and the iterative work are both real. Both are necessary. Pretending the foundation work is a sprint, cramming infrastructure provisioning and architecture decisions into story points and velocity calculations, does not make those things iterative. It just makes them harder to plan.

Know which phase you are in. Communicate that clearly to your team and your stakeholders. And when the foundation is genuinely ready, when there is something stable to build on, open the backlog, load the stories, and start moving.

Before the Next Chapter

Three things to reflect on before you move forward:

→ How does your organization's Agile practice differ from the textbook version? Make a list, not to judge the differences but to be explicit about what adaptations have been made and whether each one serves the underlying principle it was adapting.

→ Where in your current process are you in a sequential dependency situation, where certain things have to happen before others can begin? Are you acknowledging that reality in your planning, or are you trying to force iterative delivery onto a foundation that isn't ready for it?

→ Where in your current Agile practice are you following the form without the function, running a ceremony because it is on the calendar rather than because it is generating learning or alignment? What would you change if you optimized for outcome rather than compliance?

CHAPTER SEVEN

The Build vs. Buy Decision Nobody Makes Cleanly

Almost every significant product initiative inside a large organization reaches a moment where someone asks the question: should we build this, or should we buy it?

On the surface it sounds like a straightforward procurement analysis. You list the requirements, you evaluate the options, you compare the costs, you make a recommendation. Clean, rational, evidence-based.

In practice it is rarely any of those things. By the time the question reaches the table formally, vendors have usually already been in the room. Internal advocates have already formed opinions. Budget owners have already made informal commitments. Political capital has already been spent in directions that are hard to reverse. And everyone at the table has a different definition of what "cost" actually means.

The build vs. buy decision is one of the most consequential calls a product leader makes in a large organization. Getting it right requires more than a good spreadsheet. It requires intellectual honesty, a willingness to think like the people who are ultimately paying for the outcome, and the discipline to keep the real goal in front of everyone when the conversation starts to drift.

• • •

The Records Management Fight

Records management in the federal government is not a glamorous topic. Build vs. buy is also not a simple one.

Federal records management is the practice of creating, maintaining, and disposing of government records in compliance with statutory requirements, most prominently the Federal Records Act and the requirements of the National Archives and Records Administration. It matters enormously. Records create the institutional memory of an agency. They protect employees and the public in litigation. They ensure accountability and transparency. And because every program within an agency has different retention requirements, different access controls, and different compliance obligations, the records management landscape inside a large agency like CMS is genuinely complex.

When the agency began evaluating a records management solution, there was a vendor in the room early. They had been building the case for their product for some time before my team entered the conversation. They had meetings on the calendar, relationships with decision-makers, and a polished presentation that made a compelling argument for their solution. They had the leg up, as these things usually go.

What they did not have was an answer to a simple question that I kept coming back to: why couldn't we do this with what we already had?

Before you buy the most expensive solution in the room, you owe it to the organization, and to the people funding it, to evaluate the full landscape of options. In large enterprises, the answer to 'we need to buy a solution' is surprisingly often 'we already have one'—or 'there is a far less expensive one that does what we actually need.'

Rather than the expensive enterprise vendor solution being pitched, the agency had better options available. After thorough analysis, we identified a third-party records management tool that covered the substantial majority of what the agency actually needed, at a fraction of the cost of the vendor solution. It was not the flashiest option in the room. It did not have the polished demo or the established relationship with decision-makers. But it was the right tool for the job, and the numbers made that undeniable.

My team had to move quickly. We put together a formal analysis: requirements mapped against capabilities, cost comparison, implementation complexity, long-term maintenance considerations. We got in front of the decision-makers. We made the case not as advocates for our platform but as stewards of the agency's resources.

That framing mattered. I have always tried to approach these decisions from the perspective of the person ultimately paying for them. In the federal government, that is the taxpayer. When I am evaluating whether to spend hundreds of thousands of dollars, or potentially millions, on a vendor solution versus leveraging an existing capability, I ask myself honestly: if this were my money, would I make this call? That question cuts through a lot of the noise that tends to accumulate around these decisions.

Our team won that argument. The agency went with the internal solution. The cost savings were significant: hundreds of thousands of dollars, possibly more over the life of what would have been a multi-year vendor contract. And the solution worked, because we had done the analysis to ensure it would before we made the recommendation.

The lesson is not that you should always build over buy, or that vendors are always wrong. Sometimes the vendor solution really is the right answer: when the capability gap is real, when the build cost exceeds the buy cost over a realistic time horizon, when the internal team doesn't have the expertise to build and maintain what's needed. The lesson is that the decision deserves genuine analysis, not momentum. And that the organization's existing assets deserve a fair evaluation before a new expenditure is approved.

• • •

The Awards Application: When Build Becomes Its Own Problem

The records management story is about resisting the pressure to buy when building made more sense. But the build vs. buy decision runs in both directions, and I have watched build go wrong just as often as I have watched buy go wrong.

There was a workflow at the agency for employee recognition, an awards process built entirely on PDFs. Forms got filled out, printed, signed, scanned, emailed to the next person in the chain, printed again, signed again, scanned again. It was slow, hard to track, and the records it produced were difficult to manage. My team saw an opportunity to build something better. The original build took about two to three months. What it delivered was clean and functional: a digital form connected to a workflow that moved submissions from employee to reviewer to director to final repository. No more PDFs. No more email chains. Clear tracking, clear status, clean records. The office we built it for was happy. We won awards for it, which I will always appreciate for the irony.

The first enhancements were reasonable. Add a custom field here. Modify the routing logic there. Small improvements that addressed things the initial build had not anticipated. Each one made sense in isolation. Each one made the application slightly more complex. And because the SharePoint developers on the team were genuinely exceptional, the kind of developers who will build an application within an application if you let them, the work got done quickly and the results were impressive. That is when the project started its slow transformation.

Over the following years, the awards application evolved into something significantly more sophisticated than anyone had originally planned. Custom forms with conditional logic. Scoring functionality that allowed reviewers to rate submissions against criteria in real time. An automated reporting layer that aggregated scores and produced summary outputs. A full archiving system that housed the records in a structured repository. It had become, in effect, a purpose-built awards management platform built entirely inside SharePoint.

I managed enough concurrent projects that I was not in every meeting for this one. What I was in was the morning standup, where the status of every active project surfaced. And what I kept hearing, week after week, was that the awards application was still in progress. Projects on our team typically ran four to eight weeks. This one had been running for six months. That kind of timeline anomaly is a signal worth examining. When I looked more carefully, the pattern was clear: the project was not struggling. It was growing. Every sprint brought a new enhancement request. Every enhancement made sense to the business owner who was asking for it. And because the developers could build it and because the business owners wanted it, there was no natural forcing function that said stop.

This is one of the most common trajectories in enterprise product work. Nobody makes a bad decision. A simple solution, built to solve a specific problem, gradually accumulates features because everyone is responding reasonably to their local incentives: the developers are delivering what gets asked of them, the business owners are asking for things that would genuinely improve the application, and the Product Manager is not close enough to the day-to-day to catch the trajectory before it has already run long. The problem is not that customers want more. Scope creep is when the accumulation of wants drives the product past the boundaries of what the platform can reasonably support, and nobody stops to have the honest conversation about what that means.

Every time a customer asks for one more feature, they are paying you a compliment. But your job is not just to say yes to compliments. Your job is to tell them honestly when the product they are describing has outgrown the solution you are building it on.

The conversation with the business owners was one I should have had earlier. They were wonderful people, genuinely invested in building something good and facing real pressure from their own leadership to deliver a capable system. When I explained where we were, six months in with one developer fully committed and scope that had grown to a point where additional enhancements would require real trade-off conversations, they heard it. They were not resistant. They had not fully seen the aggregate picture because each individual request had seemed so reasonable.

The approach I took was the same one I try to take in most difficult product conversations: understand what the customer is trying to accomplish, explain what the development environment can realistically deliver, and give honest expectations about the gap between the two. Not the gap between what they want and what the developers could build—they could build almost anything—but the gap between what would serve the customer best and what the accumulated feature list was becoming.

They agreed to scope back. Not because they stopped caring about the features they had asked for, but because when they understood the full picture they made a rational decision. They liked the platform. It was free. The version they had was already dramatically better than what they had started with. They decided to run it as it was, keep the remaining features on a list for future consideration, and let the development team close out and move on. Sometimes the right outcome of a build vs. buy conversation is neither building more nor buying something new. Sometimes it is accepting what you have, being honest about what it can carry, and making the deliberate choice to stop at good enough.

The gap between what they wanted and what SharePoint could cleanly deliver had become significant by the time that conversation happened. More custom code meant more fragility. More fragility meant more maintenance. More maintenance meant more cost: in time, in resources, and in the risk of something breaking in a way that was hard to fix cleanly.

The honest conversation was: what were you originally trying to do, and is this still serving that goal? Sometimes the answer to that question is yes, and you find a way to keep building. Sometimes the answer reveals that the customer's needs have evolved to the point where a purpose-built tool, one designed for exactly what they are now trying, to accomplish—would serve them better than a customized workaround ever could.

That is not a failure of the original build decision. That transition is the natural lifecycle of a product that was successful enough to grow beyond its original scope. But recognizing that moment, and having the courage to name it rather than just keep adding features, is part of the job.

• • •

The 95/5 Rule

Across both of these stories, and across years of watching build vs. buy decisions get made well and poorly, I have come to think of product scope through a simple ratio. I call it the 95/5 rule, and it has shaped how I approach requirements conversations, backlog prioritization, and the question of when a solution is done.

The idea is this: ninety-five percent of what a customer needs from a product is almost always achievable within a reasonable scope, using available tools and a realistic budget. The 95 percent is the core of the problem, the primary use case, the thing that, if it works well, delivers the substantial majority of the value the customer is looking for.

The other five percent is everything else. The edge cases. The nice-to-have features. The things that would be great to have someday but are not essential to the core goal. The enhancements that sound important in a meeting but that, when you look honestly at usage data, almost nobody will use.

The customers who struggle most in product development are the ones who cannot take their eyes off the five percent. They get hung up on the exception, the edge case, the feature that would be wonderful but that is not what the product is fundamentally for. And when the five percent drives the conversation, two things happen: the core ninety-five percent gets delayed while everyone argues about the margins, and the product grows in complexity and cost well beyond what the core goal required.

Get your customer to ninety-five percent. Deliver that completely and well. Then let the remaining five percent live in the backlog as the future: the enhancements, the next phase, the things you build once the foundation is solid and proven. That five percent is not a failure to deliver. It is a roadmap.

This does not mean the five percent is unimportant. Sometimes what looks like a five percent edge case turns out to be critical for a specific user group, which is exactly why you keep it in the backlog rather than throwing it away. But it is the future, not the foundation. Build the foundation first, build it well, and then use what you learn from real usage to decide which parts of the five percent deserve to come next.

Applied to the build vs. buy decision, the 95/5 rule asks a clarifying question: does the solution you are evaluating, whether built or bought, deliver the ninety-five percent clearly and reliably? If yes, it deserves serious consideration regardless of whether it covers every edge case. If the decision is being driven by the five percent, by features that sound compelling in a vendor demo but that address scenarios most users will rarely encounter, that is a signal worth examining carefully before committing to the cost.

Think of it like buying a drill. Cheap drills break after a few uses; expensive professional-grade drills are built for daily contractor work, and a range of options in between. Most homeowners going to the hardware store do not need the contractor drill. They need something reliable, reasonably priced, and appropriate for the job they actually have. Spending three times as much for capability you will never use is not prudent stewardship. It is a failure of honest needs assessment dressed up as thoroughness.

Find the drill that gets the job done. Deliver the ninety-five percent. Keep the five percent honest. And when the product outgrows the solution, be the person who names it clearly enough that the next decision can be made well.

Before the Next Chapter

Three things to reflect on before you move forward:

→ Think about a recent build vs. buy decision in your organization. Was the full inventory of existing capabilities genuinely evaluated before the external option was pursued? If not, what drove the momentum toward buying, and was that momentum justified?

→ Is there a product or solution in your portfolio that has grown significantly beyond its original scope? Have you had an honest conversation with the customer about whether the current platform can continue to carry that growth, or are you just adding features and hoping the foundation holds?

→ Where are your customers currently focused on the five percent? What would it take to redirect that energy toward delivering the ninety-five percent well first, and do you have a clear articulation of what that ninety-five percent actually is?

CHAPTER EIGHT

Data, Metrics, and the Art of Telling the Right Story

Every year, without exception, someone in a large organization asks the same question about your program: is this still worth what we are paying for it?

In the private sector that question often comes through a quarterly review, a board presentation, or a strategic planning cycle. In the federal government it comes through the budget process: a formal, annual reckoning where programs across an agency compete for funding, where the ones that cannot demonstrate their value are cut, and where the burden of proof falls entirely on the people running the program.

For eight years managing the SharePoint program at CMS, I answered that question every single year. And the answer was never obvious, never automatic, and never just about the numbers. It was about the story the numbers told, and whether that story was compelling enough to keep the program alive for another year.

• • •

The Annual Budget Defense: A Masterclass in Applied Metrics

Federal agencies operate on a fiscal year that runs from October through September. Each year, program offices across the agency submit budget justifications: formal arguments for why their program deserves continued funding, at what level, and for what purposes. Programs that cannot make a convincing case get reduced or eliminated. The competition is real and the stakes are real.

For a program like the enterprise SharePoint platform, an internal infrastructure tool not a public-facing system and not directly tied to CMS's core mission of administering Medicare and Medicaid, making that case required deliberate, continuous measurement of everything the platform did and everything it enabled.

Help desk ticket volume told us how much active use the platform was generating and where users were experiencing friction. User counts and active session data showed the breadth of adoption across the agency's 6,000 federal employees and 3,000 contractors. Storage trends (the growth from gigabytes to terabytes over the years) showed that people were trusting the platform with more and more of their work. Project completion rates demonstrated operational throughput. Cost savings from automation initiatives gave budget reviewers a direct dollar figure they could compare against the program's cost.

None of these metrics were collected casually. They were tracked deliberately, reported consistently, and presented in formats designed for the specific audience receiving them. What a technical briefing to an infrastructure team looked like was different from what an executive budget justification looked like. The underlying data was the same. The story built from it was tailored to what each audience needed to understand and believe.

Data does not speak for itself. In a large organization, data is raw material. Your job is to shape it into a narrative that a specific audience can understand, believe, and act on. That is not spin. That is communication.

The discipline of annual budget defense taught me something about metrics that I have not seen written down anywhere: the most important metrics are not the ones that are easiest to collect. They are the ones that answer the question the decision-maker is asking. In a budget review, the question is never "how many tickets did you close?" The question is: "is this program worth what we are spending on it, and what would we lose if we cut it?" Every metric you present should be in service of answering those two questions, directly and credibly.

Over eight years, the story we built around the SharePoint platform evolved. Early on it was primarily about adoption: how many people were using it, how frequently, for what purposes. As the platform matured, the story shifted toward impact: the cost savings from automation, the reduction in manual processes, the improvement in system uptime and performance. By the time we were managing 13.5 terabytes of data across 104 site collections and 1,300 project sites, the story almost told itself. But we still had to tell it, clearly and annually, because institutional memory in large organizations is shorter than most people assume.

• • •

The Cloud Migration: When the Right Story Takes Years to Prove

The annual budget defense was a known challenge—difficult but predictable, with a well-understood audience and a clear format. The cloud migration cost justification was something harder: making a financial case for a decision whose full benefits would not be visible for two to three years, to an audience that was accustomed to thinking about cost as what they were paying right now.

CMS was among the earlier large federal agencies to move enterprise infrastructure from on-premises servers to cloud-based architecture. This was not a small decision. On-premises infrastructure means physical servers, housed in data centers, maintained by dedicated staff, with all the capital expenditure, space requirements, power consumption, and redundancy planning that entails. Moving to the cloud meant transitioning that entire physical footprint to virtualized infrastructure distributed across multiple geographic locations, with the redundancy, uptime guarantees, and scalability that modern cloud platforms provide essentially as standard features.

The long-term cost argument for cloud is well-established today. In the early days of that migration, it was much less obvious to budget reviewers who were looking at line items and seeing, in the transition period, two sets of costs: the legacy infrastructure that still had to be maintained while the migration was underway, and the new cloud costs that were ramping up before the old costs had fully ramped down. For a period of time, the migration made the budget look worse before it made it look better.

Some of the most important investments an organization can make will cost more in the short-term than the alternative. Your job is not to hide that reality. The job is to build a credible model of where the trajectory leads and earn enough trust that decision-makers are willing to follow you there.

Making that case required a different kind of data storytelling. We could not show the savings yet because they had not fully materialized. What we could show was the trend: the decreasing cost per unit of storage and compute as legacy infrastructure was decommissioned, the increasing reliability metrics as redundancy improved, the elimination of specific cost categories that on-premises infrastructure required and cloud did not. We could show analogous migrations at comparable organizations and the trajectory those programs had followed. We could model the three-year and five-year cost curves with enough rigor that the projection was credible rather than aspirational.

We also had to be honest about the complexity of the transition itself. Moving from on-premises to cloud is not simply a technical migration. It involves contract strategy: ensuring that the personnel and capabilities needed for cloud operations are covered under the appropriate contract vehicles, that recompetes are timed to support the transition rather than disrupt it, that the scope of work in existing contracts does not inadvertently constrain the new work. It involves workforce planning: identifying which staff need new skills, building those capabilities before they are needed rather than after. It involves coordination across IT, security, procurement, and program leadership that does not happen by itself.

Budget reviewers who understood only the top-line cost numbers could not evaluate any of that. The data story had to surface those dimensions of complexity, not to overwhelm the audience but to give them an accurate picture of what was being managed and what the investment was covering.

• • •

What Makes a Metric Matter

Across eight years of annual budget cycles, a cloud migration, and dozens of program reviews and executive briefings, I developed a set of principles about metrics that I want to share directly.

First: measure what matters, not what is easy. Every platform generates data. Help desk tickets, page views, login counts, storage consumed: these are available because the systems produce them automatically. But they are not always the metrics that answer the questions decision-makers are asking. Before you build your measurement framework, start with the questions you will need to answer (in budget reviews, in executive briefings, in stakeholder conversations) and work backward to the data that answers them.

Second: establish baselines before you need them. A metric that shows improvement is only meaningful if you know what it improved from. The programs I have seen lose budget arguments most often are the ones that cannot show a before-and-after because they never measured the before. Start tracking the things that matter as early as possible, even before you have a specific reason to present them, because the day will come when you need the historical trend and you cannot go back in time to collect it.

Third: know your audience and translate accordingly. The metrics that resonate with a technical team (uptime percentages, latency improvements, storage efficiency ratios) are not the same metrics that resonate with a budget reviewer or an executive sponsor. The underlying data is the same. The translation into business impact is what changes. A 99.9 percent uptime figure means something to an engineer. "This system was available and performing for all 9,000 users on 364 days out of 365" means something to a program director deciding whether to renew a contract.

Fourth: be honest about what the data does not show. Metrics can be cherry-picked. Trends can be framed to look better than they are. The product leaders who build the most durable credibility with executive audiences are the ones who are honest about limitations alongside strengths, who acknowledge when a metric is trending in the wrong direction and explain what they are doing about it, rather than hoping nobody notices. Decision-makers in large organizations have seen enough polished presentations to recognize when something is being hidden. The leader who tells the truth about the hard numbers, alongside the good ones, is the leader who gets trusted with the next difficult decision.

A metric you present honestly, including its limitations, is worth more to your credibility than ten metrics that only tell the flattering part of the story. Trust is the currency that makes data persuasive. You build it by telling the truth even when the truth is inconvenient.

Fifth, and perhaps most importantly: the story matters as much as the numbers. Data informs decisions, but it does not make them. People make decisions, people with priorities, constraints, relationships, and a limited amount of time to absorb complex information. Your job is not to present data and hope it speaks for itself. Your job is to construct a clear, honest, compelling narrative that puts the data in context, connects it to what the audience cares about, and leads them toward the conclusion the evidence supports.

That is not manipulation. It is communication. And it is one of the most valuable skills in enterprise product leadership: one that no certification course teaches, one that you develop only by doing it, examining the results honestly, and doing it better the next time.

• • •

The same data told different stories depending on who was in the room. That was not a coincidence or a compromise. It was the job.

Help desk ticket numbers are a good example. On the surface, a ticket is a ticket: someone had a problem, they submitted a request, someone resolved it. But the story that data tells changes completely depending on who you are presenting it to and what decision they are trying to make.

When I brought ticket data to a budget conversation with senior leadership, the framing was about resource allocation. Tickets trending up meant the platform was being actively used and that the support team needed adequate staffing to maintain service quality. A high volume of resolved tickets was evidence that the team was functioning and that the investment was justified. If I walked into a budget review with a chart showing ticket volume increasing year over year and no support staff to match, that was a problem. If I walked in showing tickets resolved within SLA at a high rate, that was a program worth funding. Same numbers. Different frame. Different decision.

When I brought ticket data to an internal operations conversation, to the team leads and the developers and the training coordinators, the framing was about pattern recognition. What were people actually calling about? If a cluster of tickets was coming in around a specific feature, that was a signal. If site owners were consistently asking about permissions management, that was not a support failure. That was a training gap. If end users were submitting tickets about adding a logo to a page, a simple task that any site owner should be able to handle—that was a documentation problem, not a development problem. The ticket data was showing us where our users were getting stuck, and the conversation with the team was about what to build or change in response.

The same report. The same numbers. One conversation was about funding. The other was about improvement.

• • •

The metric I came to trust most over eight years was unique users, not total hits or page views, but the number of distinct individuals accessing the platform within a given month. That number told the truth in ways that aggregate traffic numbers could not.

Total hit counts are easy to inflate. A single user accessing the same page thirty times in a month produces thirty hits. That looks like activity. A thousand active sessions from one power user is not the same as thirty different people each engaging with the platform once. When you are trying to demonstrate that a platform is genuinely embedded in how an agency works, that people across the organization depend on it, that removing it would be disruptive—unique users is the number that makes that case. Hit counts tell you the system is running. Unique users tell you the system matters.

I also learned to look at that number over the right time window. Day-level unique user data is almost meaningless for an enterprise collaboration platform. People take days off. They attend trainings. They are heads-down on a deadline and not touching the system. Month-level unique user data smooths all of that out and shows you the genuine utilization pattern. If unique users were stable or growing month over month, the platform was healthy. If they started declining, that was a signal worth investigating, not necessarily a crisis but a question that needed an answer.

• • •

The more complicated lesson about metrics came from watching how contractors sometimes reported them.

I worked with skilled, professional contractors throughout my time at CMS. Most of them were genuinely excellent and reported accurately. But in the federal contracting world, performance ratings—called CPARs (Contractor Performance Assessment Reports) carry real weight. A positive CPAR matters for a contractor's ability to win future work. That creates an incentive, sometimes a subtle one, to present metrics in the most favorable light possible.

The most common version of this was reporting total hits instead of unique users. A system showing 10,000 monthly hits sounds impressive until you ask how many unique individuals those hits represent and the answer is 3,000. The other 7,000 hits were repeat visits by the same people. That is not a fraudulent number (10,000 hits is 10,000 hits), but it is a misleading one if the audience interprets it as evidence of broad adoption.

The practice I developed was to always ask where a metric came from before accepting it as accurate. What exactly is being counted? What is excluded? What would this number look like if measured differently? That is not an accusatory question. It is a professional one. The contractors who were reporting accurately had no problem answering it. The numbers that were being presented in the most favorable framing became visible when you asked the follow-up.

Data does not lie. But it does not always volunteer the full truth either. Your job is to know the difference, ask the right questions, and make sure the story you are telling, and the story others are telling you, is built on the right foundation.

Before the Next Chapter

Three things to reflect on before you move forward:

→ What are the two or three questions that your most important decision-makers are trying to answer about your program? Are the metrics you currently track and report designed to answer those questions, or are they designed to answer questions nobody is asking?

→ Do you have baselines for the things that matter most in your program? If a budget reviewer asked you today to show improvement over the past two years, would you have the historical data to do it? If not, what do you need to start measuring now?

→ Think about the last time you presented data to an executive or budget audience. Were you translating the metrics into the language of business impact, or were you presenting technical measurements and hoping the audience would make the translation themselves? What would the presentation look like if you started with their questions rather than your data?

PART THREE
Leading Without a Mandate

CHAPTER NINE

Influence Without Authority

If you have been in product management for any length of time inside a large organization, you have encountered the central paradox of the role: you are accountable for outcomes that depend entirely on people you cannot tell what to do.

The engineers do not report to you. The vendors have their own management chains. The security team has its own priorities. The infrastructure team has its own backlog. And yet when something does not get delivered, when a timeline slips, when a dependency falls through, the accountability lands on you.

This is not a design flaw. That fragmentation is the design. Product management in complex organizations is fundamentally about creating aligned motion across people and teams you do not control. The leaders who understand this early, and who develop genuine skill at it, are the ones who build lasting reputations and lasting programs.

The foundation of all of it, every time, is the same thing: communication.

• • •

Communication Is Not a Soft Skill

I want to push back on something that gets said constantly in professional development contexts: the idea that communication is a "soft skill." The implication is that it is secondary to the hard skills: the technical knowledge, the methodology expertise, the analytical capability. Nice to have, but not where the real work happens.

That framing is wrong. Communication is not the packaging around the real work. Influence is the mechanism by which the real work gets done.

Authority tells people what to do. Communication makes them want to do it. In a complex organization where you cannot mandate anything, the second capability is worth ten times the first.

This is not about being persuasive in a manipulative sense. Communication is about being genuinely clear: about what you are trying to accomplish, why it matters, what you need from each person, and how their contribution connects to something larger than the immediate task. When people understand the why, they bring something to the work that compliance with a mandate never produces: judgment, initiative, and genuine ownership.

• • •

The 120-Person Coordination Problem

Over ten years at CMS, I coordinated work across a total of 120 vendor team members spread across six different vendor organizations, though at any given contract cycle I was typically working with one or two contract teams, with a maximum of around 45 people at a time. None of them reported to me. Getting that many people moving in the same direction, across different contracts and different leadership chains, without any formal authority over any of them, is a problem that cannot be solved by process alone.

What actually worked, over and over, was giving people a collective understanding of the work they were part of, not just their piece but the larger picture. What was the platform trying to become? Who depended on it and why did it matter to them? When people could see themselves inside a story that was larger than their individual assignment, the quality and the ownership of their work changed.

The person on your team who is causing the most friction is often the person who feels least seen. That is not always true, and it is not an excuse for behavior that genuinely needs to be addressed. But it is worth asking the question before you reach for a more forceful tool.

• • •

The Vendor Who Talks But Doesn't Move

I want to give you a specific example, because influence without authority can sound abstract until you see what it looks like in a real interaction.

A vendor pattern appears more than once, and most people who have managed contracts for any length of time will recognize it immediately: lots of talk, not much movement.

You're on a call. You raise a concern—a deadline that has slipped, a communication gap that keeps recurring, a deliverable that keeps arriving in a form that requires significant rework. The contractor's project manager listens. They acknowledge the issue. They express genuine-sounding concern. And then the call ends, and the next sprint looks exactly like the one before it.

This is frustrating in a specific way that is different from outright conflict, because there is no obvious confrontation to have. Nobody is telling you they won't fix the problem. They are just not fixing it. And so the question becomes: how do you create movement without formal authority to require it?

I learned early in my career, partly from production work where feedback loops are immediate and unforgiving, to hold my work loosely. Constructive criticism is not an attack. That friction is a signal that someone wants better, and better is what you're both trying to build. The contractors I worked with most effectively were the ones who received that feedback the same way, as information to act on and not an indictment to defend against.

But not everyone operates that way. Some contractors have been in enough environments where feedback was punitive that they have developed a defensive posture that looks like agreement and produces no change. For those situations, I found that the most effective move was not escalation to their management, which tends to create defensiveness and resentment rather than genuine correction,—but rather a request for a specific, written action plan with specific dates.

Not "we'll work on improving communication" but "by this date, we will implement this specific change, and we will know it has worked when we see this specific outcome." That specificity does two things: it makes the commitment concrete enough to track, and it reveals immediately whether the contractor is able or willing to make it. Vague commitments followed by no change are a pattern. Specific commitments followed by no change are a conversation with their management that now has documented context behind it.

The difference between a vendor relationship that produces results and one that produces activity is almost always a question of specificity. Vague agreements allow everyone to feel like they are trying. Specific agreements reveal whether anyone actually is.

A constraint worth acknowledging honestly: your instinct may be to simply direct the contractor to do things differently, and that instinct runs into a real limitation. Under FAR 1.602-2, the person with authority to direct contractors is the Contracting Officer, not the technical representative or program manager. A COR—a Contracting Officer's Representative—can monitor performance, document issues, and communicate concerns. What a COR cannot do is make commitments that change the contract's price, quality, quantity, or delivery terms, or directly supervise the contractor's employees.

What that means in practice is that influence, for a program manager working with contractors in the federal space, is not just philosophically preferable to authority. It is often the only legal option. You build the relationship, maintain the documentation, communicate clearly through the right channels, and bring issues to the Contracting Officer when the relationship alone isn't enough. That constraint, like most constraints in regulated environments, is clarifying. You know exactly what your tool is. Use it well.

• • •

The PR Side of Every Program

Every significant product initiative has a communication campaign attached to it, whether you design one intentionally or not. If you do not design it intentionally, the campaign runs itself, and the story it tells is whatever people fill the information vacuum with: rumors, anxiety, worst-case assumptions, resistance rooted in the unknown.

When we were preparing for a major SharePoint upgrade, the announcement was not just a notification. It was the opening of a conversation. Here is what is changing. Here is why. Here is what you will be able to do that you cannot do today. Here is what we need from you to make the transition smooth. Framing a system upgrade as something exciting rather than something being done to people is not spin. That framing is honest, because the upgrades genuinely did improve the experience for the people using them.

• • •

What Influence Actually Looks Like in Practice

It looks like starting every new vendor relationship with a genuine conversation about what success looks like for them, not just for the program. That conversation costs thirty minutes. The alignment it creates can last years.

It looks like being the person who shares information proactively rather than waiting to be asked. When something is changing that affects a team you depend on, tell them before they find out from someone else. Proactive transparency builds credibility faster than almost anything else.

It looks like following through, every time, on the things you commit to. Your word is your primary asset in a world where you cannot mandate anything. The leader who says they will do something and does it builds a reputation that makes every future request easier to grant.

And it looks like investing in relationships during the quiet periods, not just when you need something. The vendor you call only when there is a problem will treat you like a problem. The vendor you check in with regularly, whose success you have taken a genuine interest in, will go the extra distance when you need it.

Authority tells people what to do. It gets compliance, and compliance is sometimes enough. But the work that happens when people are genuinely aligned, when they understand the goal and bring their full capability to it rather than just their contracted hours, is a different order of magnitude.

• • •

The Intranet That Paid Back

The clearest example I have of a relationship investment returning at exactly the right moment involves the agency's intranet—and an award we eventually received for building it.

The situation began the way many of the best program opportunities do: someone else's problem created an opening. The communications team was facing a mandate to move off the platform they had been using for the agency's internal website. They needed somewhere to go. We had been investing in our relationship with that team for some time, not transactionally and not because we had a project in mind, but because building genuine partnerships across the agency was how I believed programs like ours survived over the long-term.

When the opening appeared, I approached them directly. I told them I thought we could build something together, something better than what they had been working with, at no additional cost to them, on a platform we already maintained and understood. They listened. We partnered. And over the course of several months, we built a new intranet that served the entire agency: better navigation, cleaner architecture, a system that actually functioned the way its users needed it to.

An intranet is where agency employees find their org chart, read policy updates, and understand what is happening in their organization. When everyone in the building uses something you built, it is easier to explain why your program deserves to exist.

We received an award for that project, which I am genuinely proud of. But the award was not the return on the relationship investment. The return came later, in the budget cycles.

In those annual reviews, the moments when someone in a senior position looks at a line item and asks why the agency needs to keep paying for SharePoint, we had something most programs do not have: a direct, visible, agency-wide product that people were using daily. The directors who were asking those questions were using the intranet. Their staff were using the intranet. When the communications team spoke up in those rooms about the value of what we had built together, they were not doing us a favor. They were telling the truth about a product they had helped create and that their team depended on.

That is what relationship investment actually looks like when it returns. It is not a favor called in. It is a genuine partner advocating for something they believe in, in a room where their voice carries weight, at a moment when your program needs it most. If we had only interacted with the communications team when we had something to gain from the interaction, that advocacy would never have existed. The relationship existed first. The program benefit came from the relationship being real.

Before the Next Chapter

Three things to reflect on before you move forward:

→ Where in your current program are you most dependent on cooperation that is not contractually required: a team that has to prioritize your work, a decision-maker who has to say yes, a partner who has to show up? Is that cooperation secured, or are you operating on assumption and goodwill? What would it take to make it more durable?

→ Think about your most challenging vendor relationship right now. When was the last time you asked for a specific written action plan rather than a verbal commitment to improve? What would that conversation look like?

→ Does the senior leadership above your program have an accurate picture of what it delivers, not the polished summary from the last briefing, but the real operational complexity? If they had to describe your program to someone else today, would it be recognizable? If not, that is a communication gap, and it is yours to close.

CHAPTER TEN

Coaching Up, Down, and Sideways

Mentorship has been one of the most consistent threads running through my career: first as the person receiving it, then as the person giving it, and eventually as both at the same time.

I have been lucky in the mentors I found along the way. People who saw something in me before I fully saw it in myself, who pushed me past the comfortable edges of what I thought I was capable of, who believed in my potential when I was still working up the courage to act on it. That experience shaped how I think about leadership at every level: up toward the people I report to, down toward the people I develop, and sideways toward the peers and partners I depend on.

Coaching is not a formal program. Coaching is not something that only happens in scheduled one-on-ones with a designated mentee. Coaching is a posture, a way of engaging with the people around you that is oriented toward their growth and not just their immediate utility to the program. And it is, I would argue, one of the most overlooked capabilities in enterprise product leadership.

• • •

Coaching Down: Seeing What People Don't Yet See in Themselves

The developer had been doing technical work for years when I first started working closely with him. He was good at it, genuinely skilled, well-liked by the customers he interacted with, and deeply knowledgeable about the platform in a way that only comes from spending real time inside it. His reputation among the people he supported was uniformly positive. He was the kind of person who got things done and made it feel effortless.

What I saw when I watched him interact with people was something that his job description did not require and that no one had specifically developed in him: he was relatable. He could talk to a user who was frustrated about a feature that was not working the way they expected, and within a few minutes he had them calm, understood, and confident that the problem was going to get resolved. That is not a technical skill. That is a people skill, and in an enterprise environment, it is rarer than most technical skills.

He did not see any of this in himself. He thought of himself as a developer. That was his role, his identity, and in his mind, his ceiling.

One of the most important things a leader can do is hold a larger vision of someone's potential than they currently hold for themselves, and then create the conditions that let them discover it is real.

The first time I asked him to do something outside his job description, the context was practical: we had a gap. We needed to deliver training to a group of users and I did not have enough capacity on the team to cover it with the people who normally ran those sessions. He had the product knowledge. He had the rapport. I asked him if he would take it on.

He was reluctant. Not resistant—he did not push back or say no—but you could see the hesitation. Training meant standing in front of people and talking through material in an organized way, which is a different cognitive task than solving a technical problem. Developers who know a product extremely well often find it harder, not easier, to explain it to someone who does not share their mental model. The knowledge is so embedded that it is difficult to unpack at the level of detail a new user actually needs.

We worked on it together. The early sessions were what you would expect: a little too close to the slides, a little too much ground covered too fast. The common instinct when you know something deeply is to share all of it. The harder skill is deciding what not to say, what to slow down on, where to leave space for questions. That is the thing we kept coming back to in the coaching conversations. It is not about how much you know. It is about what the person in front of you needs to walk away understanding.

He got it. Not all at once, but progressively, in the way that actual skill development happens. The sessions started getting easier to follow. The questions he got started becoming better questions, which is a signal that the audience is tracking. And then something shifted.

We had a program called Lunch and Learns, informal training sessions open to anyone at the agency who wanted to attend. No requirement, no agenda beyond a topic, just an opportunity to learn something useful about the platform. The first few sessions drew maybe forty people. Then sixty. Then ninety. We were in a rhythm, and he was a significant part of why. People were coming because the sessions were useful and because the person running them was someone they trusted.

I told him more than once during that period that I saw something in him beyond the developer role. Those were direct conversations, not performance review language or bureaucratic encouragement, but actual honest assessments of what I observed. I told him that the way he worked with people, the way he was able to make technical things feel approachable, was a capability that not everyone had and that it was worth developing deliberately if he wanted to. We talked about what a move toward more leadership-oriented work might look like, what skills would need to develop, what opportunities might be worth pursuing.

He stayed at the organization. His company recognized what I had seen and started using him more for the stakeholder-facing work, the interactions that required someone who could translate between the technical and the human. That is the kind of recognition that takes time to earn and that compounds once it arrives.

I did not make him something he was not already. What I did was name what I saw, give him room to practice it, and tell him that the thing he was doing well was worth pursuing further. That is most of what developing someone actually requires. The capability was already there. It just needed someone to point at it and say: that. Do more of that.

Pay attention to the people around you at a level beyond their current function. What do they do effortlessly that others find hard? Where do they light up? What capabilities are they carrying that their current role does not require but that a slightly larger role would? Those observations, shared directly and followed up with real opportunity, are how you develop people. Not through formal development plans alone, but through the daily practice of seeing and naming what is already there.

• • •

The New Employee Guide: Coaching Before You Have a Title

Not every coaching story involves a formal mentor-mentee relationship. Sometimes it is just about seeing a need and deciding to do something about it.

When I transitioned from contractor to federal employee at CMS, I had an advantage that most new federal hires did not: I already knew the center. I had been working there as a contractor, which meant I understood the systems, the processes, the resources, and the informal landscape in ways that someone arriving from outside could not. I remembered what it had felt like to be new and uncertain about where everything was and how everything worked, the bureaucratic complexity that is invisible to people who are used to it and genuinely disorienting to people who are not.

The formal onboarding process, the new employee orientation that everyone went through, covered the essentials. But there was a gap between what orientation covered and what people actually needed to find their footing quickly: the practical, day-to-day knowledge of how to navigate the center, access the right systems, understand the key resources, and feel like they belonged somewhere rather than just showed up somewhere.

So I built a guide. A comprehensive new employee booklet that walked through the things I wished someone had handed me, organized in a way that made the center's complexity navigable rather than overwhelming. I got leadership to sign it, which gave it credibility and signaled that the organization cared about the experience of new people arriving. And I made it available to every new hire who came through.

Coaching does not require a title or a formal program. It requires noticing where people are struggling and deciding to help, even when helping is not in your job description and nobody asked you to do it.

That guide was, in its own small way, an act of institutional generosity. It cost me time that I could have spent on other things. It returned nothing directly to me in credit or recognition, at least not immediately. But it made a real difference for the people who received it, and it built relationships and goodwill that lasted for years.

I tell this story not to suggest that everyone should go build onboarding materials for their organization, though if that gap exists where you work, someone should probably fill it. I tell it because it illustrates something about the coaching mindset that I think is easy to miss: it is not about your relationship to any specific person. It is about your orientation toward the people around you. Leaders who coach are constantly asking, at some level, what does this person need that they do not currently have, and is there something I can do about that?

• • •

Coaching Up: The Translation Problem

Of the three directions, up, down, and sideways, coaching upward is the one that makes people most uncomfortable, because it requires a kind of courage that is easy to talk about and hard to practice. You are, in effect, helping someone who has more formal authority than you to understand something they do not currently understand, without making them feel like they should have understood it already.

Over ten years at CMS, I worked with multiple directors and multiple layers of leadership above my program. Each transition brought a new person with a new vision, new priorities, and a new starting point of understanding about what the SharePoint platform actually was and did.

Here is something I observed consistently across all of those transitions: incoming leadership almost never had an accurate picture of the programs they were inheriting. Not because they were careless, but because they were responsible for hundreds of programs, hundreds of employees, and a span of organizational complexity that made genuine depth of knowledge about any single program essentially impossible. They arrived with assumptions, sometimes accurate and often not, about what each program was, what it cost, and whether it was worth what it cost.

For a program like ours, whose value was not immediately obvious and whose capabilities were frequently underestimated, that assumption gap was dangerous. A leader who thought SharePoint was just a document storage system might reasonably wonder whether it needed the level of investment it was receiving. A leader who understood it was an enterprise application platform serving 9,000 people, running critical business workflows, and generating millions of dollars in efficiency savings would ask very different questions.

My job, every time new leadership arrived, was to close that gap as quickly and clearly as possible. Not to overwhelm them with everything at once, but to give them the essential picture: what the program was, what it enabled, what it would cost the agency to lose it—in terms that connected to what they cared about as leaders. And then to keep reinforcing that picture over time, because understanding that arrives once and is never reinforced does not stick.

Leadership does not ignore your program because they do not care. They ignore it because they are responsible for hundreds of programs and they will focus their attention where the story is clearest. Your job is to make your story the clearest one in the room.

The leaders who responded best were the ones who asked questions and were willing to have their initial assumptions updated. The harder ones were the leaders who arrived with a strong prior view and treated any evidence that complicated it as a challenge to their authority rather than useful information. For those leaders, the approach had to be different—slower, more patient, finding the angles that connected our program's work to their stated priorities rather than presenting the program on its own terms and hoping they would meet it there.

Coaching upward, at its core, is about helping people in positions of authority make better decisions about the things you understand better than they do. It requires humility about the limits of your own formal power and confidence in the value of what you know. Both at the same time. It is not always comfortable. But it is always worth doing.

• • •

Coaching Sideways: Peers, Politics, and the Long Game

Sideways is the direction where organizational politics live most visibly, and where the coaching mindset is most easily crowded out by competitive instincts.

In large organizations, peer relationships are genuinely complicated. The security team, the infrastructure team, the contracting office, the program managers running adjacent initiatives, all of them are operating their own programs, managing their own priorities, and navigating their own pressures. Some of them will be natural allies. Some will be indifferent. And some, occasionally, will be actively difficult in ways that range from simply unhelpful to genuinely obstructive.

For the difficult ones, I learned over time that the first question worth asking is always: what is driving this? Sometimes a peer who seems uncooperative is simply overwhelmed with their own program and genuinely does not have capacity for yours. Sometimes they do not understand your program well enough to see why it should matter to them. Sometimes there is a history you walked into that predates your involvement. And sometimes, honestly, you are the problem: something in how you have been approaching the relationship is creating friction that a different approach would dissolve.

Starting with genuine curiosity about what is driving the difficulty, rather than frustration or escalation, solves more problems than any other tactic I have tried. Not always. Some peers will not engage no matter what approach you take, and in those cases you find other paths: different team members who have better chemistry with them, different framings that get through where direct conversation has not, or simply the patience to keep building the relationship incrementally rather than expecting it to resolve quickly.

In a large organization, the peer who seems most difficult today may be the person you need most in two years. Build the relationship anyway. The investment almost always pays off eventually, and the cost of burning it is much higher than it looks in the moment.

A specific dynamic in large organizations deserves to be named directly, because I watched it play out many times: the steamroller.

The steamroller is the peer who is primarily focused on moving up, and who treats the relationships and programs around them as instruments of that ambition. They will take credit where they can, minimize the contributions of others, and use information strategically rather than sharing it openly. They move fast and they can look impressive in the short-term.

In the federal government especially, where careers are long and institutional memory runs deep, the steamroller strategy almost never ends well. The people who have been there for twenty years remember everything. The relationships that were burned come back around. The patterns become visible to the leaders who are paying attention, and those leaders tend to be the ones whose sponsorship matters most for long-term advancement.

I was fortunate to advance in my career without taking that path. Not because I was saintly about it, but because I genuinely believed, and still believe, that transparency, generosity, and a consistent focus on helping the people around me succeed was both the right way to operate and, over time, the most effective. The reputation I built across my time at CMS was built one relationship at a time, through the accumulation of small acts of honesty and helpfulness that individually seemed minor and collectively became something that opened doors I did not even know were there.

That is the long game. It requires patience that is genuinely difficult when you are watching faster-moving people get ahead in the short-term. But in organizations where careers last decades and relationships compound over time, it is the only game worth playing.

The harder truth is that the long game requires you to keep playing it even when you cannot yet see the return. There will be relationships you invest in for years before they matter. There will be peers who burn bridges you spent time building and seem to face no consequence for it, at least not immediately. There will be moments when the patient path feels like the slow path, and you will have to decide, again, that you believe what you believe. I have had those moments. I still have them. The decision does not get easier. It just gets more deliberate.

• • •

Before the Next Chapter

Three things to reflect on before you move forward:

→ Who on your team is operating below their potential? Not because of performance issues, but because their current role does not require everything they are capable of. What is one opportunity you could create in the next thirty days that would let them show something larger?

→ Think about the last leadership transition you lived through. How quickly did you move to close the assumption gap with the incoming leader? What did you do, and what would you do differently now to make the program's value clear faster?

→ Is there a peer relationship in your current environment that is more difficult than it should be? Before you attribute it to their personality or priorities, ask honestly: what might be driving it, and is there an approach you haven't tried that might change the dynamic?

CHAPTER ELEVEN

The 115 Briefings Lesson

People sometimes raise an eyebrow when I mention that I delivered over 115 executive briefings during my time managing the SharePoint program at CMS. The implication in that look is something like: that sounds exhausting. That sounds like a grind. How did you keep going?

The honest answer is that I had a blast.

Not every single briefing, and not every single moment. But the work of getting in front of people and talking about something I genuinely believed in, showing them what the platform could do, making the case for where it was going, helping them understand why it mattered, was not a burden. It was the part of the job I looked forward to most.

Sustainable advocacy for a program comes from genuine belief in it. And genuine belief is not something you perform. Expertise is something you earn, over time, by doing the work closely enough and long enough that the program becomes part of how you see yourself.

• • •

Growing Up With the System

I spent eight years with that SharePoint program. Eight years is a long time in technology, a long time in any professional role, and a genuinely unusual tenure in a field where two or three years in a position is considered standard.

What those eight years gave me was something that cannot be acquired any other way: I grew up with the system. I was there when it was small: a few hundred gigabytes, a handful of sites, a user base that was still figuring out what the platform could do for them. I was there as it scaled into the terabytes, as it expanded across divisions and groups and eventually agency-wide, as it evolved through multiple major version upgrades and eventually a full cloud migration. I watched it become something that 9,000 people depended on every day for work that mattered.

When you have that kind of history with a program, briefing people about it is not recitation. Briefing is storytelling. You are not reading from a slide deck. You are sharing something you lived. The numbers are not statistics you memorized; they are milestones you remember reaching. The capabilities you are describing are not features you read about in a release note; they are things you fought to build and watched people discover.

The most persuasive advocate for any program is someone who has lived it long enough to speak about it from experience rather than from a slide. Institutional knowledge is not just an operational asset. That fluency is a communication superpower.

That depth of knowledge also made the briefings easy in a way that would be difficult to replicate without it. When someone asked a hard question, about cost, about capability, about how something compared to an alternative, I did not need to go find the answer. I knew the answer, because I had been there when the question was first asked, years earlier, and had watched what happened when we worked through it. That confidence is not something you can fake, and audiences know the difference.

I got into that role, originally, because someone saw what I was already doing. I was contributing vocally in user groups, pushing the program into territory it had not gone before, and someone in leadership noticed and asked me to formalize what I was already doing. That is a pattern worth noting: the best advocacy roles often find you when you are already doing the work, not when you apply for the title.

• • •

The Right Ingredients

What makes a program worth advocating for comes down to something simple: the soup either works or it doesn't.

When you have the right ingredients, a product that genuinely solves real problems, a team that is capable and committed, a user base that needs what you are building, and leadership that is at least willing to be convinced, the advocacy almost takes care of itself. You are not selling something people do not want. You are helping people understand something that is already working and showing them how much further it can go.

When the ingredients are wrong, when the product does not really fit the need, when the team is struggling, when the organizational support is genuinely absent, no amount of briefings will make it work. You can be an exceptional communicator and still be unable to sustain a program that is fundamentally not the right solution for the problem it is trying to solve.

The reason I could deliver 115 briefings without losing energy or conviction is that the soup was right. The SharePoint program genuinely worked. The value was real. The growth was measurable. Every briefing I delivered was backed by evidence I believed in, delivered to audiences who had real reasons to care, about a program that deserved their attention and their investment.

You cannot sustain genuine advocacy for something you do not believe in. The energy runs out. The conviction fades. Audiences feel the difference between someone who is selling and someone who is sharing. Find the work you can talk about forever, and then talk about it.

This connects to something I feel strongly about for anyone building a career in product management: do not chase the role or the salary first. Chase the work you can love. Because the work you love is the work you will do best, stay in longest, and advocate for most effectively. I had many days at CMS where I lost track of time entirely because the work was genuinely engaging. That is not a small thing. That is how careers become something other than just a way to pay the bills.

• • •

The Power User Group: Change from the Ground Up

Of all the things I did to build and sustain the SharePoint program over eight years, the one I am proudest of is the Power User Group, which we called PUG.

The idea behind PUG was simple, and deliberately different from what most internal IT programs do when they want to drive adoption. Most programs lead with governance. They hold meetings about policies, about what users are and are not allowed to do, about compliance requirements and usage guidelines. Those meetings are necessary, but they are not exciting. They do not make people want to use the platform. They make people feel like the platform is something that happens to them.

PUG flipped that entirely. We did not talk about governance. We talked about capability. Every other week we gathered users from across the agency and showed them something the platform could do that they probably did not know about. Workflows. Document collaboration. Automation. New features that had arrived in the latest version and that most users had never seen. We did not just show. We taught. We enabled people to build things themselves if they wanted to, and connected them to our team if they needed help building something more complex.

The goal was empowerment, not compliance. We wanted people to leave every PUG session with something they could not do before they arrived: a capability, a technique, a connection to someone who could help them solve a problem they had been carrying for months.

The fastest way to drive adoption of a platform is not to mandate it. The goal is to make people feel powerful when they use it. Give someone a capability they did not have yesterday and they will come back. Give an entire organization that experience and the platform grows itself.

And it did grow itself, in exactly the way I had hoped. It started with individuals: a single person who came to a PUG session, learned something, and built a small solution for their own use. Then that person shared it with their team, and the team wanted something bigger. The team's solution became a model for the division. The division's work caught the attention of the group level. And slowly, organically, the platform spread upward and outward through the organization, carried not by mandates from IT but by people who had experienced its value directly and wanted more of it.

That individual-to-division-to-group-to-agency growth arc is not something you can force. You can create the conditions for it. You can show up consistently, teach generously, and make it easy for people to go further than they thought they could. But the growth itself happens because the value is real and people can feel it. That is what 115 briefings and a biweekly power user group were really doing: not selling a platform, but creating the conditions for people to discover what it was worth to them.

• • •

What Sustained Advocacy Actually Teaches You

Years of briefings, user groups, executive presentations, and informal conversations about a single program taught me things about organizational change that I have not found clearly stated anywhere else.

The first is that change in large organizations is almost never the result of a single compelling presentation. Adoption is the result of cumulative exposure: the same message delivered consistently to the same people and their successors, over a period of time long enough for the message to become part of how the organization thinks. One great briefing plants a seed. A hundred briefings, sustained over years, grows a forest.

The second is that the people who resist your program most vocally are often your most important audience. Not because their resistance is correct, but because if you can win them over, or at least earn their grudging respect, you have addressed the strongest version of the objection. The people who were already on your side did not need the briefing. The skeptics did.

The third is that expertise, openly shared, is the most durable form of credibility. Every PUG session, every briefing where I answered a hard question directly and honestly, every moment where I said "I don't know, but I will find out" instead of bluffing—all of it built a reputation that made the next conversation easier before it even started. You cannot buy that reputation. You can only earn it, slowly, through the accumulation of small moments where you chose honesty and helpfulness over the easier path.

And the fourth, which underlies all the others: find the work you can believe in, and then show up for it every single day. Not because every day will be remarkable. Most days are not. But because the days add up, the work compounds, and the program you help build over eight years of consistent, passionate, honest effort becomes something that no single briefing could have created.

That is the 115 briefings lesson. It was never really about the briefings.

• • •

The first briefing I gave to senior leadership at CMS happened in my first week on the job. I had not yet fully found my footing in the program, did not yet have the institutional knowledge that would come from years of working inside it, and did not yet have the easy fluency with the material that I would eventually develop. What I had was a team member who had been there longer than me, a topic that leadership already wanted to pursue, and enough sense to let the room's momentum work in my favor.

The topic was moving to the cloud. The federal government was in the early stages of a significant shift toward cloud infrastructure, and the direction was already well established before I walked into that briefing room. In some ways, it almost did not matter how the briefing went. The destination was already decided. What the briefing needed to do was demonstrate competence and build confidence in the team that would be doing the work.

Senior leadership briefings in a large federal agency have a specific geography that I did not fully appreciate until I experienced it. You move upward—literally. From the working floors where the program teams operate, up to the floors where the office directors and deputy directors sit. The conference rooms feel different. The tables are longer. There are more people sitting along the walls, in observer chairs rather than at the table itself. And then, at some point in your tenure, you stop being one of the wall people and you become one of the table people. That transition happens gradually and then all at once, and when it happens you understand why the briefings that looked effortless from the back of the room were harder than they appeared.

I am an INTJ, one of the sixteen Myers-Briggs personality types characterized by introversion, strategic thinking, and a preference for working from a clear internal framework rather than from the energy of the room. When I tell people that at work, they are often surprised. They see someone who facilitates meetings, leads briefings, builds relationships across an organization, and they do not expect introversion. What they are seeing is a skill that was built deliberately over time, through repetition, through the accumulated discomfort of doing the thing before I was fully comfortable doing it. The first briefing was harder than the fiftieth. The fiftieth was harder than the hundredth. By the time I had given more briefings than I could easily count, the preparation was still there—I never stopped preparing—but the performance of it had become something closer to natural.

That is the thing about career capital that builds from repetition: it does not feel like accumulation while it is happening. It feels like one more briefing, one more conversation, one more time standing in a room and making a case for something you believe in. The accumulation only becomes visible in retrospect, when you look back and realize that a version of you from five years earlier would not have been able to do what you are doing now without thinking twice about it.

• • •

A less comfortable version of the briefing story is also worth telling.

Not every briefing is for something you believe in completely. Not every initiative lands in your portfolio because you championed it. Sometimes a decision gets made above you, a direction gets set by leadership, and your job becomes to carry the message into rooms where you are expected to present it with conviction.

I experienced this with senior leaders who came into the organization with their own assumptions about the platform, assumptions that were sometimes incomplete, sometimes based on experiences from different systems, sometimes simply resistant to being updated. A leader would come in from another agency, carry a frustration with SharePoint's search functionality from a previous environment into their new role, and repeat that frustration in meetings regardless of whether it reflected the current state of the system.

That kind of persistent misconception is one of the harder things to address through a briefing. You cannot argue someone out of a position they did not reason themselves into. You can offer context, invite a follow-up conversation, create an opportunity for them to experience the thing they are skeptical about directly. But if the leader is not interested in having that conversation, if the frustration is more about preference than about a genuine problem that needs solving—there is a limit to what a briefing can accomplish.

What I learned from those situations was that the briefing is not always the resolution. Sometimes it is just the moment of planting something: a piece of context, a reframe, a question that lands differently six months later when circumstances have changed. The follow-up matters as much as the room. The relationship you have built over time matters more than the slide deck you brought that day. If the person on the other side of the table trusts you as a professional, they are more likely to revisit a position. If they do not know you, they have no reason to.

The 115 briefings were not all wins. Some of them were seeds that took a long time to germinate. Some of them planted things that were harvested by whoever came after me. That is fine. The point was never the individual briefing. The point was the accumulated presence: the consistent voice in the room, the person who showed up prepared and stayed credible, who made it easy for leadership to believe in the program because they had come to believe in the person representing it.

Before the Next Chapter

Three things to reflect on before you move forward:

→ Do you genuinely believe in the program or product you are currently advocating for? If yes, what is the story of how you came to believe in it, and are you telling that story when you brief stakeholders, or are you presenting data without the conviction behind it?

→ What is the equivalent of PUG in your organization, the forum where you can show people what your product can do rather than what it requires of them? If it does not exist, what would it take to create it?

→ Think about the last time you delivered the same message to a skeptical audience and felt the energy go out of it. Was the issue the repetition, or was it the ingredient mix, something about the program, the audience, or your own belief in it that needed to be examined honestly?

CHAPTER TWELVE

When Things Break

Everything breaks eventually. Systems fail. Vendors miss. Timelines collapse. Decisions that seemed sound turn out to have been built on assumptions that didn't hold. Audiences notice when the projector goes dark at exactly the wrong moment. Thousands of users reach out at once when a server goes down and nobody has an answer yet.

How you lead in those moments, not the moments when everything is working but the moments when nothing is, is one of the truest tests of what kind of leader you actually are. And the instinct that most people bring to a crisis is almost always the wrong one.

Most people, when things go wrong, speed up.

• • •

The Mentor in the Chaos

I want to go back a long way for this one—back before the federal government, before enterprise IT, back to a megachurch in Minnesota where I was working as a media specialist and learning, without knowing it, some of the most durable lessons of my professional life.

Live production environments are unforgiving. A church service with a full sanctuary is a real-time event with no pause button and an audience that will notice every failure. When a projector lamp blows, when an amplifier fails, when a microphone starts cutting in and out at exactly the moment the pastor is making the most important point of the sermon, every eye in the room eventually finds its way to the production booth. The person running audio and video becomes, in that moment, the person responsible for everything that is wrong, whether or not any of it was within their control.

I experienced one of those moments early in my time there. It was not one thing going wrong. It was several things, arriving in quick succession, each one demanding attention while the previous one was still unresolved. A projector issue. Audio problems in the sanctuary. Equipment failures layering on top of each other while a service was either in progress or about to begin. I was running. Grabbing things. Trying to communicate in three directions at once. Diagnosing without fully diagnosing. Moving so fast that I was making the situation worse by skipping steps, missing obvious things, circling back to collect equipment I should have grabbed the first time.

My mentor watched this for a moment. And then he told me to stop.

Slow down. When everything is going wrong at once, the instinct to move faster is the instinct that will cost you the most. The person who stops, thinks, and moves deliberately will always outperform the person who sprints through a crisis without direction.

Not slow down as a figure of speech. Literally stop moving for a moment. Take a breath. Think about what the actual problem is before doing anything else. Identify the commonality if there is one: multiple failures happening at the same time often have a single root cause, and finding that cause resolves everything while chasing each symptom separately resolves nothing. And before picking up any piece of equipment, think about what else you will need so you do not have to make the same trip twice.

It sounds simple. It felt impossible in the moment. Everything in my body was telling me that speed was the answer, that action was the answer, that standing still while things were breaking was its own kind of failure.

But he was right. When I slowed down, I could think. When I could think, I could diagnose. When I could diagnose properly, the actual fixes became obvious in ways they had not been when I was running in circles.

I have carried that lesson with me through every role I have held since. And somewhere along the way, I noticed that I had internalized it so completely that my response to crisis had actually inverted: I do not just slow down when things go wrong. I go slower. Deliberately, consciously, almost counterintuitively slower, because I have seen enough times what happens when a leader loses their composure in a crisis, and I know that the team is watching and calibrating their own response to mine.

• • •

The Server Goes Down

Fast-forward to CMS. Thousands of users. An enterprise platform that people depend on for real work every day. And one afternoon, a main server goes down.

The messages start arriving almost immediately. Users cannot access the system. Work is interrupted. People want to know what is happening, when it will be fixed, and who is responsible. The volume of incoming communication is itself a kind of chaos: each message individually reasonable, collectively overwhelming, all of them demanding a response before there is anything concrete to say.

The wrong response in that moment is to react to the volume. To send a message before you know what happened. To make a commitment about resolution time before the infrastructure team has diagnosed the issue. To escalate in a way that creates more noise than clarity. All of these feel like action. None of them are useful, and several of them make the situation harder to manage once the real work of resolving it begins.

What we did instead was establish the sequence. First: confirm the infrastructure team was aware and working on it, which they were. Second: escalate to management so that the appropriate people knew an outage was in progress, not to create alarm but to ensure nobody was surprised and everyone who needed to be looped in was. Third: craft thoughtful communication to the user base. Not a rushed message full of uncertainty. A calm, clear acknowledgment that there was an outage, that the team was actively working on it, and that users would be updated as information became available.

In a crisis, your users do not need you to have all the answers immediately. They need to know that someone is in control, that the problem is understood, and that they will not be left without information. Calm, honest communication in the first ten minutes of an outage is worth more than a perfect resolution statement two hours later.

The outage resolved. They always do, eventually. The system came back. Users returned to their work. The disruption was real and the frustration was real, but the way it was managed, the escalation, the communication, the steady presence through the chaos—meant that what people remembered afterward was not primarily the failure. It was how the team handled it.

That is what crisis leadership is really about. Not preventing every failure. You cannot. Not having a perfect answer the moment something goes wrong. You will not. Leadership in a crisis is about being the steadiest person in the room when the room is at its most unsteady, so that the people around you have something to orient toward rather than a second source of chaos to manage.

• • •

What the Audience Always Knows

Something worth naming: the particular vulnerability of live production environments, whether that is a church service, an executive briefing, a product launch, or a system that 9,000 people use simultaneously. The audience always knows when something is wrong. They may not know what is wrong, or why, or whose fault it is. But they feel the disruption. They see the hesitation. They notice the gap between what was promised and what is happening.

And their instinct, in that moment, is to look for a leader. Not for someone with an immediate solution, but most audiences are reasonable enough to understand that some problems take time to fix. They are looking for someone whose demeanor communicates: I know this is happening, I am on it, and we are going to be okay.

That is a leadership act that has almost nothing to do with the technical resolution of the problem. That steadiness is purely about presence and composure. And it is available to anyone, regardless of title or formal authority, who has done the work of developing it.

The media specialist in a production booth, staying calm while the projector fails, communicating clearly to the team, prioritizing methodically rather than reacting to everything at once, that person is leading as surely as any executive in a boardroom. The context is different. The principle is identical.

• • •

The Real Question at the End of Every Crisis

I want to close this chapter with something that has stayed with me since those early days in Minnesota, sharpened by years of outages and failures and moments where programs were at risk and things were breaking in too many directions at once.

Everything does eventually work out. Not always in the way you planned, not always on the timeline you hoped for, and not always without real cost. But the crises end. The servers come back online. The briefings get rescheduled. The programs find a way forward. In my experience, that has been true more reliably than the anxious, in-the-moment version of events ever suggested it would be.

So the question is not whether things will be okay. They almost always will. The question is whether you will be okay when they are.

Will you have managed your own response to the crisis in a way that preserved your health, your relationships, and your credibility? Will the people around you have experienced you as a steadying presence or as another source of stress? Will you have slowed down enough to think clearly, communicated calmly enough to be trusted, and moved deliberately enough to actually fix the right things rather than just the nearest ones?

Those are the questions that determine what kind of leader you are. And the answers are built not in the moments when everything is working perfectly, but in the moments when nothing is, and you choose, deliberately and against your instincts, to slow down.

• • •

Years later, inside a large federal enterprise environment, I got to test that lesson under real conditions.

We were migrating a SharePoint environment from one major version to a newer one. Migrations at enterprise scale are among the more technically demanding things a platform team does. You are not just moving data. You are moving permissions, configurations, site structures, custom solutions, workflows, and the accumulated complexity of years of decisions made by dozens of different people across dozens of different projects. Before the migration, we had taken snapshots of everything. We had the before state documented. We had scripts ready. We had a plan.

What we did not fully anticipate was a permissions failure on the other side.

The discovery came through help desk tickets: a cluster of users suddenly unable to access things they had been accessing the day before. The access was there in the source environment. It had not transferred cleanly to the destination. The contractor team flagged it. The call got made. And everyone who needed to be on that call was on it quickly.

The energy in the room was not panic. It was confusion, a specific kind of confusion that comes when something that should have worked did not work and nobody yet knows exactly why. That kind of confusion has a way of accelerating into blame if the first person to speak makes it about accountability rather than resolution. I had seen that happen in other contexts. Speculation in a crisis is rarely useful and almost always slows things down.

My first move was not to establish what went wrong or who was responsible. My first move was to slow the conversation down and establish a unified plan. I brought the lead people together: the technical leads, the project lead, the people who had the deepest knowledge of what the scripts had done and what the expected outputs were supposed to look like. We looked at what we had. We compared the before snapshots to the current state. We identified the scope of the permissions gap. And then we assigned the remediation work systematically, using the ticketing system to track each piece so nothing fell through.

That is the lesson from the church in Minnesota, applied to enterprise IT: stop before you sprint. The instinct when something breaks is to move faster, to grab things, to be seen doing something. The professional habit, the one that takes years to build, is to pause long enough to understand the actual problem before you start solving it. In most cases, five minutes of clear thinking saves an hour of frantic activity.

The fix took a few hours. We worked through the help desk tickets that had come in, identified the users who were affected, and communicated directly to those stakeholders rather than sending a broad communication that would create more confusion than clarity. The team stayed calm throughout. When I left CMS, one of the things a colleague mentioned in a farewell note was that I had a habit of remaining calm under pressure. I was glad to hear that because I had worked at it deliberately. Calm is not a personality trait. Composure under pressure is a practiced response.

What changed after that migration was our validation process. We added spontaneous, randomized permission checks across site collections, not just at the end of a migration but at intervals throughout, so that if something was not transferring correctly we would catch it before users did. We also built a more rigorous comparison process between the before and after states, not just running a report but actually validating that the outputs matched what was expected.

Every failure teaches something if you are paying attention. The permissions issue taught us that a completed script is not the same as a verified outcome. Those are different things, and treating them as the same thing is exactly the kind of assumption that produces a calm Tuesday morning crisis.

Before the Next Chapter

Three things to reflect on before you move forward:

→ Think about the last time something went wrong on your watch. What was your instinctive response, to speed up or to slow down? Looking back, what would the slower, more deliberate version of your response have done differently, and what would the outcome have been?

→ What does your crisis communication look like in practice? Do you have a sequence (confirm, escalate, communicate) that you follow consistently, or do you react to the volume and urgency of incoming messages without a clear order of operations?

→ How do the people around you experience you when things go wrong? Are you the steadying presence in the room, or are you adding to the noise? This is worth asking someone who has seen you in a crisis, because your own perception of your composure is almost always more flattering than the reality.

PART FOUR
Building a Career That Travels

CHAPTER THIRTEEN

The Government PM Advantage Nobody Talks About

A perception problem follows federal and government-adjacent workers into the private sector job market, and it is worth naming directly before anything else in this chapter: a lot of hiring managers do not know what to do with a federal resume.

They see the agency name and think: slow. Bureaucratic. Risk-averse. They see the tenure, eight years in one role, and wonder whether someone who stayed that long can adapt to a faster-moving environment. They see the scope described on paper and struggle to calibrate it against private sector equivalents because the reference points are unfamiliar. A $35 million portfolio, 120 vendor team members, 9,000 users, 13.5 terabytes of data: these numbers are real and they are large, but they do not come with a private sector translation built in.

That translation gap is your problem to solve. Not because your experience is insufficient: it is more than sufficient, in most cases more extensive than what a comparable private sector role would have produced. But because the burden of making your value legible always falls on the person who holds it, not on the audience that needs to understand it.

This chapter is about that translation. And it starts with being honest about what federal service actually is, for the people who have done it and the people who are trying to evaluate it from the outside.

• • •

What People Get Wrong About Government Work

The stereotype of the federal worker is someone coasting toward a pension, protected by civil service rules from any real accountability, moving slowly through a system that rewards longevity over performance. Like most stereotypes, it contains just enough truth to be misleading and enough distortion to be genuinely unfair.

The federal workers I know, the ones I worked alongside for nearly a decade at CMS, are among the most mission-driven professionals I have encountered in any sector. They are not there for the money, because the money is not what brings people to public service. They are there because they believe in the mission. At CMS, that mission is administering healthcare programs—Medicare, Medicaid, the Children's Health Insurance Program—that collectively serve over 150 million Americans, many of them among the most vulnerable people in the country.

When I went to work every day at CMS, I was working for those people. Not in an abstract, inspirational-poster sense. In a direct, operational sense. The systems I managed served the employees and contractors who administered those programs. If our platform failed, their work failed. If our platform improved, their ability to serve beneficiaries improved. That connection to mission is not something you have to manufacture at a federal agency. The slowness is structural, built into what the organization exists to do.

Federal workers are not slow because they lack ambition. They operate carefully because the stakes are real, the accountability is public, and the people depending on the work are often the people who can least afford for it to go wrong.

I left federal service during a period of genuine institutional disruption: a time when remote work policies were being reversed, when reductions in force were affecting people across agencies, when the stability that had been one of public service's defining features was no longer guaranteed in the ways it once had been. The decision to leave was about my family first. But it was not a decision I made lightly, and it was not one I made because I had stopped believing in the work.

What I carried out with me was ten years of experience that the private sector, I quickly discovered, did not fully know how to read. And so I had to learn how to translate it.

• • •

The Scale Argument

Let me start with the most straightforward part of the translation, because it is the one that surprises people most once they actually look at the numbers.

Managing an enterprise SharePoint platform at CMS meant managing a system that served 9,000 concurrent users (6,000 federal employees and 3,000 contractors) across an agency whose work affected the healthcare of more than 150 million Americans. The data footprint grew from gigabytes to terabytes over the course of my tenure. The project portfolio at its peak ran to thousands of active items. The contract I managed had a total value of $35 million and involved coordinating 120 vendor team members across six separate vendor organizations.

Very few private sector companies operate at this scale in their internal enterprise systems. The ones that do are large enough that the comparison is immediately credible. The ones that do not are often surprised to discover that a federal IT program was running at dimensions that dwarf their own internal technology operations.

Scale matters because scale is where the hard problems live. Managing a backlog of 50 items is a different skill from managing 3,000. Coordinating a team of eight is a different skill from coordinating 120 across six vendors with different contracts, different management chains, and different organizational cultures. Running a platform for 200 users is a different challenge from running one for 9,000 users who depend on it for real work every day.

The federal PM who has operated at genuine enterprise scale has developed muscles that cannot be built in smaller environments. They have encountered the full complexity of dependency management, stakeholder coordination, vendor accountability, and organizational politics at a level that most private sector roles simply do not require. That is an advantage. It needs to be named as one.

• • •

The Compliance and Patience Dividend

Here is one that takes longer to explain but may be even more valuable in practice: federal workers understand compliance, bureaucracy, and the patience required to operate within both, at a level that most private sector professionals have never had to develop.

Data retention in the federal government is not a two-year policy. Depending on the record type and the program, retention requirements can run five to seven years, or longer, or in some cases permanently. The governance frameworks are not suggestions. The security requirements are not optional. The procurement processes are not something you can route around because your timeline is tight. Every decision of consequence runs through a series of reviews, approvals, and documentation requirements that would feel suffocating to someone who had never navigated them and that become, over time, simply the terrain for someone who has.

That patience, the ability to work methodically within a system that was not designed for speed, to build the relationships and the credibility that allow you to move as efficiently as the system allows, to stay focused on the goal while the process takes as long as it takes, is genuinely transferable. Regulated industries in the private sector have compliance environments that are demanding in their own ways. Large enterprises have internal bureaucracies that can be just as complex as government ones. Healthcare, financial services, pharmaceuticals, defense contracting: all of them place premiums on the kind of patient, process-aware, compliance-fluent leadership that federal service develops almost by necessity.

The federal PM who can navigate bureaucracy without losing their mind is not demonstrating a tolerance for dysfunction. They are demonstrating mastery of one of the most complex operating environments that exists. That mastery transfers directly to any large, regulated, high-stakes organization.

When I moved to my current organization—a pharmacy benefits management company operating in a regulated healthcare environment—I did not experience the compliance requirements as foreign or burdensome. I recognized them. The specific rules were different, the agency was different, the mission was different. But the underlying discipline of operating carefully within a framework of requirements designed to protect people and manage risk, that was entirely familiar. It was what I had been doing for a decade.

• • •

The Translation Toolkit

Understanding the value of your federal experience is necessary but not sufficient. You also have to know how to make that value legible to audiences who do not share your frame of reference. Here is what I have learned about doing that effectively.

Lead with impact, not process. Federal resumes are often written in the language of process: what you did, how you did it, what framework you used. Private sector hiring managers want to know what changed because of your work. The $1.8 million in cost savings. The 90 percent improvement in user engagement. The migration that completed six months ahead of schedule. Start there, and then explain the context if you need to.

Translate the numbers explicitly. Do not assume that $35 million or 120 vendor team members will self-evidently communicate scale to someone who has not worked in a federal context. Draw the comparison directly: this is the equivalent of managing a mid-sized technology company's entire internal platform budget. This is the coordination complexity of a multi-vendor outsourcing arrangement of the kind that large enterprises use for their most critical systems. Make the private sector analog explicit rather than leaving it to the reader's imagination.

Claim the regulated industry expertise. Healthcare IT, government technology, financial systems: these are not niche backwaters. They are some of the most complex, high-stakes technology environments that exist, and experience in them is directly relevant to any organization operating under significant regulatory oversight. Frame it that way, because that is what it is.

Name the mission orientation without being precious about it. Spending a decade working toward a mission you believed in is both a signal of character and a practical differentiator. People who work for reasons beyond the paycheck bring something to an organization that is genuinely hard to find and genuinely hard to manufacture. You do not need to be self-congratulatory about it. But you should name it, because it is real.

• • •

What nobody tells you about leaving a federal job after a decade is that the job market has changed in ways you did not notice because you were not in it. I had not applied for a position in ten years. The mechanics of how you find work, how you present yourself, how applications actually get evaluated, all of it had shifted in ways that were not immediately obvious, and that created a genuine learning curve on top of the more visible challenge of translating federal experience into private sector language.

The first wall most federal job seekers hit is invisible: applicant tracking systems filter resumes before a human being ever sees them, and they filter based on keywords. A resume dense with accurate federal language can score poorly against a job description that uses different terminology for the same work, not because the experience is insufficient but because the vocabulary does not match. A federal program manager who ran a thirty-five-million-dollar portfolio and coordinated a hundred and twenty vendor team members has done exactly the work large private sector organizations are looking for. But if the resume calls it a "contract portfolio" and the job description says "program governance" or "vendor management," the system may never surface it for human review. Learning to read a job description as a vocabulary guide, and then using that language in your materials rather than the language you used internally, is one of the most practical adjustments you can make, and one of the least intuitive ones.

The transition also carries a psychological dimension that deserves honest acknowledgment. When you have been in one role for a decade and you step back into a job market that no longer operates the way you remember, the early silence is disorienting. The lack of callbacks reads as rejection even when it is often a mechanics problem: resume format, keyword gaps, timing. It can start to feel like the problem is you when it is usually the problem is the translation. Those are different problems with different solutions, and keeping them distinct matters more than it sounds.

Preparation helped more than anything else. I used AI tools to run mock interviews, working through likely questions against specific job descriptions, training myself to answer in outcome terms rather than process terms. Federal experience is naturally described in process language: what we implemented, how the governance worked, what framework we used. Private sector hiring conversations respond to a different register: what changed, what improved, what the measurable result was. Retraining that instinct takes deliberate repetition, and it is worth doing before you are in a room with a real hiring manager rather than after.

I applied to roughly two hundred positions over the course of my search: across healthcare, consulting, technology, and federal contracting organizations that understood the government context. I customized every application. I also learned that timing is not a minor factor: positions at target organizations can receive hundreds of applications within the first forty-eight hours of posting. If you are not among the first applicants, your resume may be reviewed only if the initial pool does not surface strong candidates. The role I ultimately accepted had over two hundred applicants. I was among the first to apply, with a document written specifically for that opening.

The conversations that went best were the ones where I could feel the room recalibrate. A question would come in carrying an implicit skepticism, some version of can someone from a federal environment actually keep up here, and the answer would land, and the energy would shift. That shift almost always came when the specifics were concrete enough that the hiring manager had to revise their assumptions. They had arrived expecting to make allowances. They were leaving with a different picture. The move that made it happen was consistent: get to a number quickly. Thirty-five million dollars, nine thousand users, a hundred and twenty vendors, ninety-five percent on-time delivery. Numbers travel across context in a way that organizational descriptions never quite do. Once the scale was established, the conversation could move to what the scale required, and those capabilities are exactly what large organizations are looking for.

Not every conversation ended in an offer, and not every offer would have been the right one. Some company cultures revealed themselves clearly enough in the interview that the decision was easy. Part of a good search is interviewing the organization at the same time it is interviewing you, asking about working models, decision-making, how disagreement gets handled, and being willing to act on what you learn. The goal is not to get any job. The goal is to get to the right place.

The translation work is real, and it takes longer than most people expect. But the experience on the other side of it, the decade of scale, complexity, compliance, and mission—is genuine and hard-won. Do not let the friction of the translation convince you that the underlying capability is insufficient. It is not. It is, in most cases, more than enough.

• • •

What Left With You

When the federal workers who were displaced in recent years entered the private sector job market, the people who received them, the hiring managers and the organizations doing the interviewing, got access to something they may not have fully recognized: a cohort of highly educated, deeply experienced, mission-driven professionals who had been tested by one of the most complex operating environments that exists and had come through it with capabilities that are genuinely rare.

Entry-level federal positions require a four-year degree. Senior positions require more. The certification requirements are real and they are enforced. The accountability is public in ways that private sector accountability rarely is. The scale, the compliance complexity, the multi-vendor coordination, the cross-functional leadership without formal authority, all of it is genuine preparation for the hardest problems that large organizations face.

I am proud of my federal service. I am proud of what the team built, proud of the mission we served, proud of the skills and the character that decade of work developed in me. Leaving was the right decision for my family at the right time. But what I carried out the door was not a resume full of government jargon. It was a decade of hard-won capability that belongs to me, travels with me, and applies wherever I choose to take it next.

If you are a federal or government-adjacent professional reading this chapter, I want you to hear that clearly. What you have built in public service is real, it is substantial, and it is more portable than the market sometimes makes it feel. The translation work is yours to do. But what you are translating is worth the effort.

Before the Next Chapter

Three things to reflect on before you move forward:

→ Write down the three most impressive things about the scale or complexity of your federal or enterprise experience: the numbers, the scope, the coordination challenge. Now write the private sector analog for each one. Practice saying those translations out loud until they feel natural.

→ Where in your resume or your interview answers are you leading with process instead of impact? Identify two or three places where you can replace a description of what you did with a statement of what changed because you did it.

→ What regulated industry or large enterprise environment would most value the specific compliance fluency and organizational patience you developed in your government role? Are you targeting those environments—and if not, why not?

CHAPTER FOURTEEN

Certifications, Credibility, and What Actually Moves the Needle

Certifications come with a lot of noise and not enough signal.

On one side you have the credential maximalists, people who believe that the right combination of letters after your name will open any door, that certifications are the primary currency of professional advancement, and that the more you accumulate the more valuable you become. On the other side you have the credential skeptics, people who believe that real-world experience is the only thing that matters, that certifications are mostly box-checking exercises, and that anyone worth hiring can see past a resume to what someone actually knows.

Both of these positions are wrong, and the truth between them is more practical and more nuanced than either camp tends to acknowledge.

Here is where I actually land after years of accumulating credentials, using them in the job market, and watching how they function in the organizations and hiring processes I have moved through: certifications are a tool. Like any tool, their value depends entirely on whether you are using the right one for the job, whether you actually know how to use it, and whether you understand what it can and cannot do for you.

• • •

What Certifications Actually Do

The first function certifications serve is practical: they get you past the algorithm. Applicant tracking systems scan for keywords, and certifications put those keywords on your resume. If a posting asks for a SAFe POPM and you have one, the ATS finds it. If it asks for a Scrum Master certification and you have PSM II, the ATS finds it.

The most qualified candidate in a job search is not always the one who gets the interview. The candidate who gets the interview is the one whose qualifications are visible to the process that controls access to it. Certifications make your qualifications visible. That is their first and most immediate job.

Beyond the algorithm, certifications serve a second function: they provide a shared vocabulary. When a hiring manager sees SAFe POPM on a resume, they do not have to wonder whether you know what a PI Planning event is, or whether you understand the relationship between product vision and team backlog. A baseline of shared knowledge implied by the credential reduces the cognitive work of evaluating you. That is valuable, especially in early-stage interviews where you have limited time to establish credibility.

And the third function, the one that I think matters most over the long arc of a career, is that certifications, pursued with genuine intent to learn, actually teach you things. This sounds obvious but it is worth stating clearly, because there is a meaningful difference between someone who earned a certification by genuinely engaging with the material and someone who found the answer key online and passed the exam without absorbing anything. The former has a tool they can use. The latter has a word on their resume.

• • •

The Learning Mindset Behind the Credential

I am a believer in continuous learning, and I say that not as a platitude but as a description of how I have actually approached my career. Each certification I pursued was attached to something I genuinely wanted to understand better: a framework I was being asked to implement, a methodology I was seeing in job descriptions, a technology area I wanted to develop competency in.

The SAFe certifications came because I was living in SAFe environments and wanted to understand the framework deeply enough to implement it intelligently rather than just perform it. The Microsoft and Google certifications came because I was working in those ecosystems and wanted the structured knowledge that formal learning provides alongside hands-on experience. The Databricks fundamentals came because data and analytics capabilities were increasingly relevant to the product work I was doing and I wanted a baseline understanding of the space.

That sequencing, learning attached to real need and certification following genuine engagement, is the approach I would recommend to anyone building a credential strategy. Not because the credential itself requires genuine learning to be earned (sometimes it does not), but because the credential without the learning is a liability. You will be asked about it. You will be expected to apply it. And the gap between what your credential implies and what you actually know is something that becomes visible very quickly once you are inside an organization.

A certification you earned without learning is a debt you will eventually have to repay. The interview question you cannot answer, the implementation you cannot explain, the situation where your credential implies expertise you do not have, these are the interest payments. Learn first. Certify second.

The SAFe framework's principle of continuous improvement has always resonated with me personally for this reason. The idea that growth is not a destination but a practice, that the right orientation toward learning is perpetual rather than episodic, describes how I have tried to approach my own development. Not "I need to learn this for the job I have right now" but "I want to understand this because the world is moving in this direction and I want to move with it."

The rotary phone analogy is real. The people who did not learn to use a cell phone did not just miss out on convenience. They were progressively excluded from the infrastructure of modern life. The people who do not engage seriously with artificial intelligence, with cloud-native development, with the evolving landscape of digital tools and methodologies, will face a similar exclusion, not immediately but gradually, as the gap between what they know and what the market requires widens beyond their ability to close it quickly.

That is not a reason for anxiety. That reality is a reason for intentionality. Decide what to learn. Learn it genuinely. Certify when the credential adds value. And keep going.

• • •

Building a Credential Strategy That Actually Works

So how do you decide what to certify in, when, and at what level? Here is the framework I would use if I were starting from scratch today.

Start with the market, not the catalog. Look at actual job postings in the roles and industries you are targeting. What certifications appear consistently? Which ones appear in the must-have column versus the nice-to-have column? That frequency data tells you where the market is placing value right now, which is the most relevant signal available. Frameworks that were dominant five years ago may have lost ground. Emerging certifications in new areas may be appearing with increasing frequency. The market tells you this if you read it carefully.

Prioritize current over historical. Waterfall project management certification is not where you want to focus your credential energy right now, not because waterfall is worthless but because the market has moved. Agile, SAFe, cloud platforms, AI literacy, data fundamentals: these are the areas where the market is placing consistent value and where certification signals genuine current relevance. Understand the historical methodologies: knowing what waterfall is and why it exists makes you a better Agile practitioner. But certify in the direction the market is moving, not the direction it came from.

Do not let cost be the only filter. Some valuable certifications are expensive. The PMP is time-consuming and costly, and there are real debates about whether its return on investment still justifies the investment in an Agile-dominant market. But "expensive" is not the same as "not worth it," and "cheap" is not the same as "valuable." Evaluate cost against the specific doors a credential opens in the specific market you are targeting. For some roles and some industries, the PMP still matters enormously. For others, it has been largely replaced by Agile credentials. Know your market before you make that call.

Use free resources to learn before you pay to certify. The amount of high-quality, freely available learning content on virtually every relevant topic is staggering. YouTube channels, documentation, community forums, open-source tools you can actually use and experiment with, all of it available to anyone with internet access and the willingness to engage with it seriously. If you cannot afford a certification right now, learn the material anyway. Play with the tools. Join communities of practice. Build the knowledge, and certify when the credential becomes the right investment for where you are in your career.

The credential signals the knowledge. But the knowledge is what you actually bring to the work. Build the knowledge first, with whatever resources you have access to, and the certification becomes a verification of something real rather than a claim about something hypothetical.

And find your people. One of the most underrated components of professional development is the community that forms around shared learning. Other practitioners working through the same material, asking the same questions, running into the same implementation challenges, that community is where a lot of the most valuable learning actually happens. Find it. Join it. Contribute to it. The relationships you build there will serve you long after any individual certification has expired or been superseded.

• • •

The Credential Is Not the Point

I use Agile at home. That is not a joke and it is not an exaggeration. The principles of clear communication, iterative progress, honest retrospection, and shared understanding of the goal, these are not methodologies that belong only in a, professional context. They are ways of thinking about how to get things done with other people, and they apply wherever you are trying to get things done with other people.

My kids are my toughest customers. And yes, I have found that understanding how to communicate with a difficult stakeholder, to understand what they actually want rather than, what they say they want, to find the version of yes that serves both of us, to stay calm when the conversation gets frustrating, translates more directly to parenting than I ever, expected when I was sitting in a certification course.

That is what genuine learning does. It does not stay in the box you put it in. It spreads into the way you think, the way you approach problems, the way you engage with the people around you. A certification that produces that kind of learning is worth far more than the credential it awards.

The credential opens the door. What you actually know and who you actually are is what keeps you in the room. Build both, continuously, and the career takes care of itself.

• • •

Before the Next Chapter

Three things to reflect on before you move forward:

→ Pull up five current job postings for the role you want next. What certifications appear most frequently? Which ones are in your portfolio already, and which ones represent a genuine gap worth closing in the next six to twelve months?

→ For each certification you currently hold, ask honestly: did you learn the material, or did you pass the exam? Where the answer is the latter, identify one practical thing you can do in the next thirty days to close the gap between what your credential implies and what you actually know.

→ What area of emerging relevance—AI, cloud architecture, a specific platform, a new methodology—are you currently most behind on? What free resource could you engage with this week to start closing that gap, regardless of whether a formal certification follows?

CHAPTER FIFTEEN

The Pivot

My journey is not over.

I want to start there, because everything that follows in this chapter has to be understood in that context. This is not a retrospective from someone who has arrived at a destination and is looking back with the settled wisdom of completion. This is a report from the middle of the road, from someone who has covered a lot of ground, learned an enormous amount, and has no idea yet where the next lily pad will be.

That uncertainty does not worry me. It used to. It doesn't anymore.

• • •

The Full Arc

I was a flight dispatcher at a local airport before any of this. That is where the professional story starts, if you are keeping score, not in a government agency, not in a technology company, not anywhere that would obviously connect to where I ended up.

From there I started volunteering in audio-visual production at a megachurch in Minnesota, which turned into a job, which turned into one of the most formative experiences of my professional life. The mentors I found there, the technical director who taught me not just how to run a production but how to lead people, how to know when someone needs help and how to recognize when the journey is theirs alone and you cannot walk it for them, those lessons have stayed with me across every role I have held since.

Through connections made in Minnesota I landed a Technical Director role in Chicago, leading volunteer teams at a large megachurch and eventually helping orchestrate the expansion of that church into multisite campuses. The executive producer there, the mentor I have mentioned earlier in this book, pushed me into things I did not know I was capable of. She saw something in me before I saw it in myself, and she created the conditions that let me discover it was real.

Then my journey took a turn I did not plan. I moved to Baltimore, where I installed command centers for the federal government. Learned the detailed mechanics of technology infrastructure from the ground up. Ran a command center as a contractor. Got hired as a federal employee working in fraud prevention at CMS, protecting the integrity of programs that serve hundreds of millions of Americans. Became a user of SharePoint, the system I would eventually run. Got noticed for the passion and knowledge I was bringing to that platform. Joined the SharePoint team. Met remarkable people, built remarkable things, spent a decade growing a program from a few hundred gigabytes into something that touched the working life of 9,000 people every single day.

Then I left. Not because I wanted to leave (I loved that work and I loved the mission), but because the environment shifted in ways that made the decision the right one for my family. I joined a pharmacy benefits management company, still in healthcare, still building things from the ground up, still doing the work I am built for.

And somewhere in the middle of all of that, I got a pilot's license.

A career is not a ladder. A career is a series of lily pads: each one a landing, each one a launching point, the destination never fully visible until you are almost there. The goal is not to plan the perfect sequence. The skill is to jump well, and to trust that the next pad will hold.

Flight dispatcher. Audio-visual volunteer. Media specialist. Technical Director. Command center installer. Contractor. Federal employee. Product manager. Pilot. And now, whatever comes next.

That is not a resume with a clear narrative arc. That arc is a life lived with curiosity, willingness, and the consistent belief that the skills built in one place will find their use in another, even when the connection is not immediately obvious.

• • •

What the Lily Pad Life Actually Requires

I have a way of thinking about career transitions that has served me well, and it comes from an unlikely source: a pond.

Think about a frog moving across a pond on lily pads. The frog does not know exactly where it is going when it starts. It cannot see every pad from the bank. It knows the general direction, across the pond toward the other side, but the specific path reveals itself one jump at a time. Each pad is a stable landing, a place to gather yourself, assess what you can see from here, and decide where the next jump goes.

That is how I have experienced my career. Not as a plan executed across decades, but as a series of deliberate jumps, each one made from a place of genuine preparation and genuine willingness to land somewhere new. Flight dispatching taught me operational thinking and the weight of real-time decisions. The megachurch years taught me leadership, live production, and the kind of calm under pressure that my mother modeled as an EMT and that I have called on in every crisis since. The federal years taught me scale, compliance, strategic communication, and the patience that complex organizations require. The private sector taught me how those skills translate, what they look like without the federal context, and what the holistic picture of a full career begins to look like.

None of it was wasted. None of it was a detour. Every pad was exactly where I needed to land to be able to see the next one.

• • •

The Pilot's Framework for Career Decisions

When you are flying an aircraft, you always have a plan A. Your filed flight plan, your intended route, the destination you are pointed toward. But every pilot also flies with alternatives (options B, C, and D) because the sky does not always cooperate with your intentions. Weather changes. Equipment indicates something unexpected. ATC reroutes you. The pilot who has only planned for plan A is not prepared to fly. The pilot who has thought through the alternatives before they are needed is the one who makes good decisions under pressure.

I think about career pivots the same way. You should always have a plan A: the direction you are pointed, the role you are building toward, the next lily pad you are aiming for. But you should also have genuine alternatives, thought through in advance, so that when the environment changes (and it will change, it always does) you are not making a panicked decision from a position of no options. You are choosing between prepared alternatives from a position of relative stability.

This is not the same as lacking commitment to plan A. The opposite is true. The pilot who has thought through alternatives is more committed to getting where they are going, not less, because they have done the work to ensure that unexpected obstacles will not stop them. They may arrive by a different route. They will arrive.

The prepared pivot is not an admission that your plan was wrong. A go/no-go decision is an acknowledgment that the world is larger than your plan, and that good judgment means knowing how to navigate when the two come into conflict.

When I left federal service, it was not a panicked jump. It was a decision made from a position of preparation: certifications built over years, a network developed across a decade of genuine relationship-building, a clear-eyed assessment of what skills I had and where they would be valued. The pad I jumped to was a pharmacy benefits management company, still in healthcare, still building enterprise technology solutions, still doing work that connects to a mission I believe in. Plan A had changed. The direction of travel had not.

• • •

What the Pivot Taught Me About Skills and Identity

When you make a significant career transition, you discover something that catches a lot of people off guard: you are more than your role.

When I left CMS, part of what I was leaving was an identity that had been built over a decade. Senior Product Manager. SharePoint program lead. The person who had grown that platform from nothing into something that served 9,000 people. That identity was real and it was earned, and leaving it behind, even by choice and for good reasons, had a weight to it that I did not fully anticipate.

What the transition revealed was that the skills, the knowledge, the capabilities I had built, those did not belong to the role. They belonged to me. The ability to manage a complex program. The ability to communicate across the full range of organizational stakeholders. The ability to build genuine relationships with vendors and colleagues and leadership. The ability to stay calm when things broke. The ability to tell the story of a program's value clearly enough that people would fight to protect it. None of that lived in my badge or my job title. It lived in me, and it traveled with me when I walked out the door.

The private sector did not know exactly what to do with a federal resume. That is true and I have talked about it at length in the previous chapter. But once I was inside an organization, once the work started and the capabilities became visible, the translation happened naturally. The skills were recognizable. The value was demonstrable. The person who had spent a decade becoming good at something difficult was still that person, in a new context, doing similar work for a different kind of organization.

That is what a career that travels looks like from the inside. Not a seamless transition where everything is immediately obvious and comfortable. A period of reorientation followed by the gradual recognition that what you built in one place is genuinely useful in another, and that the usefulness compounds over time as the new context adds dimensions to your understanding that the old one could not have provided.

• • •

The People Who Made It Possible

I do not want to close this chapter, or this part of my story, without naming the people who made it possible. Not because it is the gracious thing to do (although it is), but because I genuinely believe that the human infrastructure of a career is as important as the professional infrastructure, and that acknowledging it honestly is part of telling the truth about how careers actually work.

My father has been in technology his entire career—a Technical Program Manager III who builds things from the ground up, who modeled what it looks like to approach complex problems with patience and precision and genuine craft. My mother spent years as an EMT, staying calm in moments of genuine crisis, helping people who needed help in their most vulnerable moments. Both of them gave me things I have drawn on in ways I did not fully recognize until I was deep enough in my own career to trace the threads backward.

The mentors at the church in Minnesota. The executive producer in Chicago. The colleagues and leaders at CMS who believed in the program and in me. The people who gave me opportunities before I had fully earned them and then trusted me to grow into those opportunities. The colleagues at Prime who welcomed someone coming from a very different context and made space for what I was bringing.

And my wife — who has been steady through every version of this career, who has never once made me feel like the work wasn't worth doing, and who is the reason any of it has meant something beyond the work itself.

You will not get where you are going alone. Nobody does. The question is whether you are paying enough attention to recognize the people who are helping you along the way, and whether you are being the kind of person who helps others in return. That is not a career strategy. That is just how a good life works.

• • •

To the Person Standing at the Crossroads

If you are reading this chapter because you are standing at your own pivot point, considering a change, recovering from one that was, made for you, trying to figure out what comes next after a career that looked one way for a long time and now looks different, I want to say something directly to you.

The skills you have built are yours. They travel. The institutional context that housed them may be gone, but what you learned, what you developed, what you became in the process of doing difficult work in complex environments, none of that was left behind when you walked out the door. It is in you. It will be visible to the right people in the next place, once you find the language to make it legible.

The pivot is not a failure. Every career transition is a jump. The next pad is out there. You may not be able to see it yet from where you are standing. That is okay. Point yourself in the right direction, do the preparation, and jump.

Not everything will be perfect. The path will not be straight. You will land on some pads that were not quite what you thought they would be and launch from them toward something better. You will meet people who help you in ways you did not expect, and you will help people in ways you will not always see.

Your career is not over. Your career is exactly as far along as it needs to be, given everything that brought you here.

Keep going.

• • •

Before the Next Chapter

Three things to reflect on before you move forward:

→ Map your own lily pads. Every role, every significant transition, every place you landed and launched from. What did each one give you that the next one needed? What is the through-line that connects them, even if it was not visible at the time?

→ What are your plans B, C, and D right now? Not as a sign of wavering commitment to where you are headed, but as a pilot's honest preparation for the conditions that will inevitably differ from the forecast. What are you building, maintaining, and keeping warm as alternatives?

→ Who are the people who made your career possible? Have you told them? If not, that is something worth doing, not for any strategic reason but because the people who believed in you before you fully believed in yourself deserve to know what that meant.

CHAPTER SIXTEEN

The Distributed Team Problem Nobody Solves Cleanly

Remote work is not a technology problem. Most conversations about it, in organizations, in policy debates, in the endless discourse about productivity and presenteeism—treat it as if better tools and tighter policies are the answer. They are not. Remote work is a leadership problem. And the leaders who figure that out are the ones who make it work.

I have been working in some version of a distributed environment for most of my career. I was among the second wave of employees at CMS to be approved for remote work, an early adopter in a large federal agency where the standard assumption was still that work happened in a building. The rest of my team was in the office. I was not. And that experience, being the remote person on an otherwise in-person team, taught me things about distributed work that you cannot learn when everyone is in the same situation.

• • •

When You Are the Only One on the Call

The problem with being the only remote person on an otherwise in-person team is not the technology. The technology was imperfect, this was before the tools and practices of the pandemic era, when videoconferencing infrastructure was still inconsistent and not everyone had a reliable audio setup, but the technology was not the real problem. The real problem was the hallway.

Decisions were made in hallways. Not formally, not in meetings with agendas and documented outcomes, but in the thirty-second conversation between two people walking from one conference room to another. Someone would mention something to a colleague, the colleague would agree, and by the time the full team was back on a call, the decision had been made, or at least pre-made, without me. Not maliciously. Not even consciously. Just because that is how proximity works. Information flows through the people who share physical space, and if you are not in that space, you are downstream.

The symptom was a phrase I heard more than I wanted to: 'just so you know.' As in: 'Just so you know, we decided this morning to go a different direction on that.' The 'just so you know' is the linguistic signature of a decision that has already been made and is now being communicated rather than discussed. That silence is the sound of being left out of the process while still being nominally included in the team.

The remote worker who is only informed rather than included is technically a member of the team and functionally a spectator. That gap does not close on its own. It has to be built closed, deliberately, by the leaders who understand what remote work actually costs when it is done carelessly.

My response to this was not to complain about it—though I understood it well enough to be frustrated—but to build structure around the gap. Recurring meetings at consistent times, so that the default cadence of communication ran through channels where I was present. Direct relationships with key colleagues, cultivated intentionally rather than allowed to develop through proximity. A discipline of reaching out proactively rather than waiting to be included. Remote work, when it is working, is deliberate in a way that in-person work does not have to be.

• • •

What COVID Changed

When the pandemic arrived and everyone moved home, something shifted that I had been trying to articulate for years. The hallway conversations stopped. Not because anyone decided to stop having them, but because there were no hallways. Everyone was suddenly on the same terms: remote, dependent on the same tools, unable to make decisions in proximity. The playing field leveled in a way I had not anticipated.

I am not going to romanticize what was a genuinely difficult period for most people and organizations. But from a distributed work perspective, something important happened: the technology caught up. Multiple platforms matured simultaneously. Video became standard rather than exceptional. Audio quality improved. Suddenly every meeting had a clear record, a visible roster of participants, a shared screen. The 'just so you know' problem did not disappear, but it became harder to sustain, because the infrastructure for including everyone had become the default infrastructure for doing anything at all.

What also became visible, in a way it had not been before, was how much leadership capability had been hiding behind proximity. Leaders who were effective in person because they could be physically present, could read the room, could pull someone aside for a quick word, those leaders sometimes struggled when the only thing they had to work with was what they communicated deliberately. And leaders who had always communicated with precision, who had always been explicit about expectations and transparent about direction, made the transition almost seamlessly. Remote work did not create the difference. It revealed it.

• • •

The Relationship You Have to Build on Purpose

In an office, relationships form incidentally. You eat lunch with someone, you take the same elevator, you overhear a conversation that leads to a connection you would not have made otherwise. None of that happens remotely. Whatever relationships exist in a distributed team exist because someone built them on purpose. If nobody builds them on purpose, they do not exist.

In What Every Body Is Saying, Joe Navarro, a former FBI counterintelligence agent who spent decades studying nonverbal communication, makes a point that remote workers feel viscerally: somewhere between 60 and 80 percent of human communication is nonverbal. When you remove the visual channel, you lose more than convenience. You lose a primary mechanism through which trust is built and maintained. You cannot see if someone is engaged.

You cannot tell if a decision landed well or poorly. You cannot read the room if there is no room to read.

This is not an argument against remote work. That reality is an argument for being honest about what remote work removes, so that you can deliberately replace what it takes away. We tried to do this in several ways: mandatory cameras on calls where relationship-building was a goal, team events scheduled before major planning cycles, informal check-ins that were explicitly not about status, deliberate conversation at the top of meetings where people could surface something other than their work agenda. None of these were perfect. All of them helped.

The team that only meets to transact will eventually feel transactional. Cohesion is not a byproduct of proximity. It is a practice. And in a distributed team, it is a practice that requires leadership.

Remote relationships have a specific vulnerability: the new team member problem. When someone joins an existing team in person, they are absorbed by the environment: they meet people in the kitchen, they overhear conversations that give them context, they pick up cultural norms by being in the room where the culture lives. When someone joins remotely, none of that happens unless you create it intentionally. Onboarding a remote hire requires more structure, more explicit attention, and more time from more people than onboarding an in-person hire. Organizations that do not understand this produce remote employees who feel isolated and disoriented, who take much longer to become effective than they should, and who often conclude within the first year that the organization does not actually care about them.

• • •

The Political Moment

I am not going to make this political. But I am going to be honest about what happened.

When the administration changed and the direction on remote work began to shift inside federal agencies, the uncertainty was real. I lived four or five hours from my CMS office. The prospect of being required to return, to commute that distance regularly or stay in a hotel during the work week—was not abstract. It was a concrete change to my family's life. And the pace and clarity of communication about what the policy would actually require was not, let's say, its best attribute.

What I observed in myself and in colleagues during that period was a phenomenon I think is worth naming: the difference between what the work required and what the policy required started to feel like a meaningful distinction. The work was the same. My output had not changed. The relationships I had built with my team, carefully and over years through deliberate effort, were functioning. And yet the conversation was no longer about the work. It was about presence, about optics, about something that felt disconnected from actual performance.

Remote work reveals something about leadership that proximity can let organizations ignore: when you manage by presence, by the comfort of seeing people in chairs, you are not actually managing performance. You are managing appearances. Those are not the same thing, and the difference eventually matters.

I made a decision to protect what mattered most to me: my family, my stability, my ability to do work I was proud of in an environment where I could do it well. I found a new position, fully remote, with a private sector organization. I left something I had genuinely loved. That was not easy. But I also walked away with something important: confirmation that the skills I had built, the capabilities I had developed over years of managing complex programs in a regulated environment, traveled. They did not require a specific building or a specific organization. They were mine.

• • •

What Remote Work Forces You to Become

The last thing I want to say about distributed work is what it has taught me about leadership that I do not think I would have learned as quickly in an office.

When you manage remotely, you cannot rely on presence. You cannot walk over to someone's desk and read their body language to assess how a project is really going. You cannot tell by looking at the room whether your message landed. You have to ask. You have to be explicit. You have to build the kind of communication infrastructure that in-person environments allow you to be lazy about, because the environment itself is doing some of the work for you.

In that sense, remote work is a forcing function for precision. You communicate more clearly because you have to. You give more explicit feedback because ambiguity travels badly over text and audio. You document decisions because the alternative is chaos. You build relationships on purpose because they do not form on their own. You are, in some meaningful sense, more intentional about everything, because if you are not, nothing happens.

I also found, consistently, that my productivity as a remote worker was higher than it had been in an office. Not because I was working longer hours (though I sometimes was), but because I was not spending twenty minutes walking between conference rooms on a campus large enough to require real transit time between meetings. I was not interrupted by the ambient noise of an open floor plan. I was not pulled into conversations I had not scheduled. When I was working, I was working. That intensity, sustained across a full day, is something the office environment genuinely interrupts.

The knock on remote workers—that they are not really working, that they are watching television and taking long lunches while their employers pay for their time, is, in my experience, almost perfectly backwards. Remote workers often cannot turn it off. No physical separation exists between where you live and where you work. The laptop is always there. The notifications do not stop at 5:00 PM the way they stop when you close a building behind you.

The people I have known who struggled with remote work struggled not because they worked too little but because they could not figure out when to stop.

That boundary—between work and the rest of your life—is something remote workers have to build for themselves, deliberately, just like everything else. Nobody gives it to you. But for those who manage to build it, what you get on the other side is a way of working that can accommodate talent from anywhere, that can survive disruption, that does not depend on everyone being in the same building to function. In a world that keeps changing in ways nobody fully predicted, that resilience turns out to matter quite a lot.

• • •

Before the Next Chapter

Three things to reflect on before you move forward:

→ Think about the last important decision that was made in your organization without the full team present. Who was included, and who found out afterward? What structure would have ensured broader inclusion, and does that structure exist yet?

→ If you manage remote or hybrid team members, how deliberately are you building their relationships with the team? What would onboarding a new remote hire look like if you designed it specifically for the isolation problem, rather than assuming proximity will solve it?

→ What does your current work environment let you be lazy about that you would have to be explicit about if your team went fully remote tomorrow? Name it. Then ask whether being explicit about it would actually serve your team better.

CHAPTER SEVENTEEN

The Tool You Cannot Afford to Ignore

An easy version of this chapter exists, and I am deliberately not going to write it. One version says artificial intelligence is going to transform everything, that Product Managers who do not adapt will be left behind, and that the future belongs to those who embrace the change. All of that is probably true in some form. But it is also the kind of thing that sounds important and is easy to forget, because it does not tell you anything specific about the actual experience of working alongside AI in an enterprise environment right now.

So let me tell you about that instead.

What AI Actually Does in Practice

I use AI every day in my current work. The most useful thing it does, the thing I would give up last if I had to choose, is take meeting notes. That probably sounds mundane. That description is not accurate. In a role where I am simultaneously facilitating a meeting, updating Jira in real time, actively listening to technical conversations between engineers, and processing the implications of what I am hearing for the product roadmap, I cannot do two things at once. Taking notes and actively listening are competing demands. When I am writing down what someone said, I am not fully hearing what they are saying next. When I am tracking the conversation, I am not documenting it with the fidelity it deserves.

The AI takes notes. I listen. And because I am listening, really listening, I can ask the intelligent questions, catch the implication sitting underneath what someone just said, and notice the moment a stakeholder's energy shifts.

Beyond note-taking, I use AI to draft user stories, refine acceptance criteria, build outlines for documents I then write myself, edit communications before they go out, and work through problems where I need to think out loud and have something respond usefully. It helps me learn things faster. It helps me extend my thinking when I am stuck. It helps me produce better first drafts of things that I then shape into what they actually need to be.

What it does not do is replace judgment. It does not tell me which features to prioritize or which vendor to trust or which stakeholder relationship is the most important to invest in right now. It does not read the room. It does not notice that the tone of a particular meeting has shifted in a way that suggests the real concern has not been named yet. It does not understand that the person who said yes in the meeting is the same person who has historically been the last to commit when things get difficult, and that the yes therefore requires a follow-up conversation before it can be treated as a commitment. Those things require experience, pattern recognition, and human judgment. They are not going away.

• • •

The Concern Is Real. The Answer Is Not Resistance.

I have had conversations with developers who are genuinely worried about what AI means for their careers. The concern is not irrational. I have built functional applications using conversational AI-assisted development that would have required a skilled developer and significant time just a few years ago. The tools for generating code from natural language prompts are advancing faster than most people expected. If you are a developer whose value is primarily in writing code that others have already specified, the competitive pressure from AI is real and it is going to increase.

What I tell people who are worried is this: the answer is not to resist it and it is not to panic. The answer is to get ahead of it by understanding what it can do and positioning yourself around what it cannot. Developers who are learning how to build with AI, how to evaluate AI-generated code, how to design systems that incorporate AI capabilities, and how to manage AI tools as part of a development workflow are not competing against AI. They are becoming the people who know how to use it. That is a much better position.

The same logic applies to Product Managers, Scrum Masters, and business analysts. The technical parts of the role, generating documentation, drafting templates, synthesizing large volumes of information into structured outputs, are going to get easier and faster with AI assistance. The human parts of the role, sitting with a stakeholder and understanding what they are really trying to accomplish, navigating the organizational dynamics that determine whether a good idea gets implemented or dies in committee, building the trust that makes hard conversations possible, are not going to change.

I think about this through the lens of what happened when other major technology shifts arrived during my career. When cloud infrastructure became accessible, the people who got ahead were not the ones who could tell you theoretically why cloud was important. They were the ones who had actually worked with it, who had made the mistakes and learned from them, who could speak with the specificity that only comes from real experience. AI is the same shift at a larger scale and a faster pace. The specificity will be earned by doing, not by reading about it.

• • •

What the Next Five Years Will Compress

Five years from now, the job market will look different in ways that are difficult to fully predict. Certain roles will shrink. Certain capabilities will become table stakes rather than differentiators. The pace of change in AI model capability has been faster than most forecasts anticipated, and there is no particular reason to expect that pace to slow.

What I am confident about is that the human interaction layer, the work of understanding what people need, building the relationships that make collaboration possible, navigating the ambiguity that lives between what a stakeholder says they want and what they actually need, is not going to be automated. You cannot automate the lunch. You cannot automate the conversation that happens when someone has been holding something back for three weeks and finally says the real thing. You cannot automate the judgment call that comes from knowing an organization's history and reading a situation in real time.

AI can help you prepare for those moments. It can help you document them afterward. It can help you synthesize what you learned and structure it into something actionable. But the moments themselves, the human moments that are the job, those are still yours.

The most consistent thread I have found across all of the AI conversations I have had with colleagues, with younger professionals, with people who are nervous and people who are excited, is this: the people who are going to do well are not the ones who are the most technical about AI. They are the ones who are the most human about everything else. The technical parts of the job will get easier. Double down on what AI cannot do. Make your communication clearer. Make your relationships stronger. Make your judgment more reliable. Those investments compound in ways that no model update will ever obsolete.

• • •

What I Would Tell Someone Starting Today

My advice to a Product Manager starting their career today is the same advice that has always been true, with one addition. Learn the fundamentals: how to understand what users actually need, how to make decisions under uncertainty, how to build alignment across groups with competing interests, how to communicate clearly and honestly at every level of an organization. Those things do not change.

The addition: learn AI. Not deeply, not as an engineer. But functionally. Know what it can do. Know what it cannot do. Use it regularly enough that you understand its strengths and its failure modes. Because there will be a moment in your career, probably sooner than you expect, when someone asks whether your product should integrate AI capability, and you need to be the person in the room who can answer that question thoughtfully. Not someone who read about it. Someone who has actually worked with it.

Knowledge has always been one of the most portable assets a professional can carry. The specific knowledge that matters is changing. Make sure you are carrying the current version.

• • •

What Building With AI Actually Taught Me

One version of the AI story stops at productivity: at meeting notes and faster emails and better first drafts. That version is true as far as it goes. But it does not go far enough.

The fuller version includes what happens when you take those tools seriously enough to build something with them.

I built a travel application called Roamara. Not as a work project, not as a proof of concept to present to a stakeholder, but because I genuinely needed it. I travel frequently, I think in systems, and I had spent years cobbling together itineraries across a half-dozen different tools that did not talk to each other. So I decided to build something that did.

Roamara is a fully functioning application. It organizes trips, checks flight status, includes a travel assistant, has chat features built in, and does the kind of itinerary management that I was doing manually for years. I actually used it when I traveled to Europe, used it to time out plans, find locations, stay on, top of logistics in real time. It worked. Not perfectly, but genuinely. I built it entirely through vibe coding, and it took me about seven months from first prompt to working product.

Seven months sounds long. In the context of what I was building, it was not. The models I was using in the early months of that project are not what they are today. They were less capable, less reliable, and required significantly more back-and-forth to get from an intention to a working implementation. What I was trying to build went from a simple trip organizer to something genuinely complex: flight integrations, a payment layer, customer accounts, mobile and desktop capability. The ambition outpaced the early tooling, and I had to grow into both simultaneously.

The most important thing vibe coding taught me was how to prompt. That sounds obvious in retrospect. It was not obvious in practice.

Early in the Roamara build I learned this the hard way. I wanted to change the background color of a settings bar. I told the AI to make the settings bar white. What I got back was an application that was mostly white, not just the settings bar but significant portions of the interface that had nothing to do with what I asked for. The AI had interpreted a broad instruction broadly, as it will do, and produced a result that was technically responsive to what I said and completely wrong relative to what I meant.

That experience reshaped how I communicated with the tools from that point forward. A good prompt is not just a description of what you want. A guardrail is a set of constraints around what you do not want changed. A guardrail is an acknowledgment that you have a working application with real customers and a payment layer and dependencies, and that the change needs to be surgical rather than sweeping. The more specific the instruction, the more surgical the result. Learning that, really learning it through repeated experience rather than just reading about it—is what separates someone who dabbles in vibe coding from someone who ships something.

I eventually moved the Roamara development out of the all-in-one platforms, the ones that will holistically rebuild your application and push changes automatically—and into a more direct workflow using a single AI to help me make targeted updates, manage the repository, and troubleshoot specific problems. The all-in-one tools are powerful for getting started. They become a liability when your application is complex enough that a sweeping automated change can break something that was working. At that point you need precision, and precision requires a different approach.

I also built two iOS applications (Five Minute Plays and Pretend Quest) through the same process. Each one taught me something different about the limits and capabilities of building with AI as a non-developer. iOS development has its own toolchain requirements, its own production environment constraints, and its own security considerations that a purely browser-based application does not. Building across those different contexts gave me a practical education in what the tools actually do well and where the human judgment cannot be delegated.

Security is the one that most people underestimate. When you are building something that handles customer data (accounts, payment information, personal itineraries) you have an obligation to think about how that data is protected. There are prompts that help with this. There are patterns to follow. But the AI will not automatically make your application secure any more than it will automatically make it functional. You have to ask the right questions and know enough to evaluate the answers.

I am not a developer. I have some coding background, enough to understand what I am looking at when I read a codebase and enough to know when something looks wrong. But I could not have built Roamara in a traditional development environment on my own. What vibe coding gave me was access to a capability that previously required a team, and what my product management background gave me was the ability to translate a complex vision into something buildable, iterate through failures without losing the thread, and ship something that actually functions in the real world.

That combination of domain expertise and AI capability is what I think the next generation of enterprise PMs will need to develop.

Not developer-level technical depth. Not blind reliance on AI to figure things out. The ability to use the tool precisely, prompt it well, and know when to trust the output and when to interrogate it.

• • •

Not everyone is there yet. Not even close.

When I talk to peers and colleagues about AI adoption, what I hear most often is not hostility. It is inertia. People have a way of working that has served them reasonably well, and adding a new tool to that workflow requires an investment of time and attention that feels like a cost before it pays off. The value is not obvious until you have used it enough for the patterns to become fluent. Most people quit before they get there.

I have also heard the skepticism that sounds like principle but is really discomfort. That using AI is somehow cutting corners. That the work should take as long as it takes. I do not think that argument holds. Every generation of productivity tooling has faced the same objection, and every generation has moved past it. Nobody says you are cutting corners by using a spreadsheet instead of a ledger.

The security community is a legitimate exception. I have spoken with security specialists who genuinely will not put sensitive information into an AI tool, and I understand that position. When your job is to think about attack surfaces and data exposure, skepticism about any third-party system handling sensitive inputs is not irrational. It is professional. That skepticism is earned, and the tools have not yet fully addressed the concerns that underlie it.

The generational pattern I have observed is real but not absolute. The people I see closest to retirement are the least likely to invest in new tooling, which makes rational sense from a return-on-investment standpoint even if it creates a gap in organizational capability. The people earlier in their careers are more likely to be using AI in some form: reviewing code, getting unstuck on a problem, drafting something faster. The ones who are getting the most out of it are treating it less like a search engine and more like a collaborator: giving it context, iterating on the output, and staying in the conversation long enough to get something genuinely useful.

One thing I wish I had understood earlier is context management. An AI conversation degrades over time. The longer a thread runs, the more the model is managing, and at some point the quality of responses starts to slip, the answers become less precise, the suggestions start to repeat. I have learned to start fresh threads more aggressively than my instinct would suggest, and to carry the important context forward explicitly rather than assuming the model is tracking everything from two hours ago. The tool works best when you treat each session as a focused engagement with a clear objective, not as an ongoing relationship with a long memory.

• • •

The Harder Problem

Five years from now, I think the enterprise Product Manager's job will look different in ways that are hard to fully anticipate and recognizable in ways that matter.

The routine will get faster. Workflows that currently require a developer's involvement will be within reach of someone with domain expertise and good prompting skills. Documentation that takes a day will take an hour. Analysis that requires pulling multiple sources together will be faster to synthesize. The administrative overhead of the job, the part that is necessary but not the reason anyone went into product management—will compress.

What will not compress is judgment. The ability to walk into a room where there is no obvious right answer and make a defensible call. The ability to read a stakeholder's actual concern behind the stated one. The ability to hold a team together through a hard quarter. The ability to decide what matters when everything feels urgent. Those things require experience, pattern recognition, and the kind of contextual understanding that comes from being present in an organization over time. AI will support all of them. It will not replace any of them.

There will be a period, and I think some organizations are already in it, where the efficiency gains from AI lead to headcount reductions that turn out to be premature. The work that looked automatable will turn out to require human judgment in ways that were not visible from the outside. Some of those organizations will hire back. Others will learn to build leaner teams that are more capable per person, which is probably the more durable model.

The harder challenge, and the one I think about more, is epistemological. We are already in a world where it is genuinely difficult to know whether an image is real or generated, whether a piece of writing was drafted by a person or a model, whether the confidence with which something is stated reflects actual knowledge or a well-calibrated hallucination. That problem does not get easier as the tools improve. It gets harder. The skill of knowing what to verify, knowing what questions to ask of a confident-sounding output, knowing when to trust your own judgment over a tool's synthesis—that is not a technical skill. The harder problem is a human one.

The enterprise Product Manager who thrives in that environment will be the one who uses AI fluently enough to get the efficiency gains, honestly enough to catch the errors, and wisely enough to know what the tool cannot do that the job still requires.

That is not a different version of the job. That future role is a more demanding version of the same one.

Before the Next Chapter

Three things to reflect on before you move forward:

→ What AI tools are available to you in your current work environment? If you are not using them, what is the actual barrier: access, comfort, uncertainty about where to start? Name it specifically, because a named barrier is one you can address.

→ Think about the parts of your job that feel most repetitive or administrative, the things that take time but do not require the judgment and relationship knowledge that make you specifically valuable. Those are the places to start with AI assistance.

→ What is one thing you have been meaning to learn about AI but have not gotten to? Commit to spending two hours with it this week. Not reading about it. Actually using it.

CONCLUSION

The Work Was Always the Point

It is Christmas. The sanctuary holds thousands of people. Outside, the winter dark has settled in the way it does in the Midwest, early and complete, the kind of cold that makes the warmth inside feel like a gift before the service has even started.

On stage: fifty actors. A live band. Lighting rigs aimed at precise angles across a set that took weeks to build. Five stage hands stationed in the wings, ready to move people and equipment on cues measured in seconds. Four cameras, each one assigned to specific shots in a sequence that had been rehearsed until it was muscle memory. A thirty-page script. A twenty-minute Christmas production that six months of development and more than a month of rehearsal had been building toward.

And somewhere in the back, at the technical director's station, me.

The lights go to black. The cues begin.

What followed was twenty minutes that I will never forget.

Rapid-fire cues to every department simultaneously. Camera shots called and cut with precision. Stage left and stage right moving at the same time, stagehands gliding through the dark with the quiet efficiency of people who have run this so many times that the choreography lives in their bodies. Lights rising and falling on cue. Video rolling on cue. Angels arriving on cue. A story unfolding on that stage, a story about a gift, about good news, about something worth celebrating, as it had been designed to unfold, exactly as all that preparation had made possible.

Things went wrong. They always do. Small things, invisible to the audience, managed in real time by people who had prepared for exactly that possibility. The production did not stop. The story did not stop. The experience that 9,000 people had that Christmas season, in the room and online, was seamless. Joyful. Exactly what it was supposed to be.

And when the lights faded to dark at the end, when the last cue was called and the last camera cut and the band played the congregation into the sermon, I sat in the back of that room and felt something that I have only ever felt in production.

It is joy. It is relief. It is the specific satisfaction of a thing done well that only the people who built it can fully understand. The audience experienced something beautiful. They did not know my name. They did not know I was there. And that was exactly right.

The unseen professional does not do the work for the recognition. The work is the recognition. The moment when everything runs exactly as it should, that moment is yours, whether anyone says your name or not.

Someone at another church I help out with gave me a nickname that has stayed with me: the silent ninja. The person in the background, making things happen, not looking for applause. I have always taken that as a compliment. Not because visibility doesn't matter—it does, and this entire book has been about how to build it strategically when it serves the work. But because at the center of everything I have described in these pages is a person who is motivated, fundamentally, by the work itself. By the thing working. By the service going well. By the system staying up and the program surviving and the team delivering and the product reaching the people it was built for.

That motivation is what sustains a career across decades and pivots and crises and the long slow grind of large organizations that move at their own pace regardless of how urgently you need them to move faster. That satisfaction is what kept me going through 115 executive briefings and eight years of SharePoint program budget cycles and every migration and upgrade and vendor negotiation and leadership transition. Not the recognition, though recognition came. The work. Always the work.

• • •

What Enterprise Product Management Actually Is

I have been asked, over the years, to explain what I do to people who are not in the industry. Not in job interview language. Not in the language of a resume. Just: what is it?

The best answer I have found is this: enterprise product management is conducting an orchestra.

Not a school orchestra. Not a weekend ensemble. The London Symphony. A world-class professional organization with dozens of specialists, each of them expert at a single instrument, all of them capable of producing something remarkable on their own, and none of them capable of producing what they produce together without someone standing at the front, holding it all in their head, and pointing.

The double bass section is your infrastructure team. You feel their contribution more than you hear it. They establish the low, foundational tone that everything else sits on top of. Remove them and the entire piece loses its grounding, but they rarely get named in the program notes.

Your senior developers are the first violins. They carry the primary melodic line. They handle the most technically demanding passages, set the pace and standard for the rest of the section, and when something goes wrong they are the ones the conductor looks to first. Alongside them, your junior developers are the second violins: essential harmonic support, learning the repertoire, developing toward first chair. The section needs both, and the first chairs are responsible for the second chairs in ways that go beyond just playing their own part well.

Your business analysts are the violas. This is the instrument that is most frequently underestimated and most acutely missed when it is absent. The violas live in the middle of the harmonic range, translating between what the melody is doing and what the bass is doing, providing the connective tissue that holds the arrangement together. A product team without strong business analysis produces the musical equivalent of a piece where the top and bottom are playing in different keys.

Your UX designers and graphic designers are the woodwinds: the oboe, the flute, the clarinet. They bring color. They bring texture. They bring the moments in a piece that make an audience lean forward without quite knowing why. Technical execution can be precise and still be lifeless; the woodwinds are the reason it is not. Their contributions are sometimes brief. They are never unimportant.

Your Scrum Master is the concertmaster—the principal first violin, seated closest to the conductor, who serves as the bridge between the podium and the orchestra. The concertmaster is not conducting. They are playing. But they are also watching, translating, keeping time when the ensemble drifts, and providing the real-time coordination that the conductor cannot provide alone at the tempo a performance demands.

Your help desk is the percussion section. They keep the rhythm. Steady, consistent, present in every movement even when they are not the loudest voice in the room. The audience almost never thinks about the percussion until something goes wrong. And then, suddenly, it is the only thing they hear.

You, the Product Manager, are the conductor. You do not play an instrument. That is not a limitation. It is the role. Your job is to hold the entire score in your head, to know what every section is doing and what they need from every other section, and to make the decisions in real time that keep a complex, living, human system moving together toward something coherent.

A single movement of a symphony has a beginning and an end. So does a product release. So does a migration. So does a project. The orchestra stops, the audience responds, and then, after the briefest pause, the next movement begins. The players are the same. The conductor is the same. The music is different. That is what enterprise product management looks like across a career: one cohesive performance after another, each one complete in itself, each one building the capability that the next one will require.

• • •

What Bureaucracy Will Try to Do to You

I have watched a lot of talented people come through large organizations and leave before they figured it out. Not because they were not capable. Because the bureaucracy got them.

It gets people in a specific way. They are working on something that matters to them. They are invested in it. And then, because of a policy decision, or a management change, or a shift in administration, or a budget cycle that did not go the way anyone expected, it goes away. And they go away with it, or shortly after, because they cannot separate the work from the specific project, the specific program, the specific version of the thing they were building.

I want to say something directly to the person who is in that moment right now, or who recognizes it from a previous version of their career: the bureaucracy is not the enemy. Bureaucracy is the environment. And the people who survive and build things that last inside large organizations are the ones who learn, eventually, that patience and the bureaucracy are in a long-term relationship, and the patient ones win.

Things will not always go the way you want them to go. Some of what you build will get cancelled. Some of what you advocate for will get overruled. Some of what you are most proud of will be replaced by something you did not ask for, for reasons that have nothing to do with the quality of what you built. That is not failure. That is the environment. Stay in it long enough and you will understand the difference.

But here is what I also want you to know: if it is genuinely not working—if the environment has become one where your contribution cannot land, where the structure is actively preventing the kind of work you came to do, there are other places. Other organizations. Other programs that need exactly what you know how to do. The skills you have built do not live in the building. They live in you. They travel.

The federal government taught me things about scale, about compliance, about stakeholder management under genuine pressure, about what it means to be accountable for something that 9,000 people depend on, that I could not have learned anywhere else at the pace I learned them there. And when it was time to leave, those things came with me. Every one of them.

• • •

What I Want You to Know That You Did Not Know on Page One

We have covered a lot of ground in this book. Bureaucracy and stakeholders and roadmaps and backlogs and metrics and influence and mentorship and crisis and credentials and pivots and distributed teams. If you have read this far, you have spent a significant amount of time inside the experience of enterprise and government product leadership as I have lived it, and I am grateful for that.

But I do not want you to leave with a list. You have had sixteen chapters of frameworks and reflections and before-the-next-chapter questions. What I want to give you at the end is simpler than any of that.

Slow down. Not just in a crisis, though especially in a crisis. In general. In the rush of large organizations and demanding programs and competing priorities and the relentless pressure to move faster, the person who can slow down enough to think clearly, communicate honestly, and make deliberate decisions will outperform the person who is always running. Every time. The mentor who told me to stop and breathe in that production booth in Minnesota was right, and I have been proving him right in every environment I have worked in since.

Be persistent. The work that matters in large organizations is almost never finished quickly. It compounds over time, like a reputation or a relationship or a program that started as a few hundred gigabytes and became something that touched the working lives of 9,000 people. Show up consistently, do the work honestly, and trust that the accumulation is building something even when you cannot see it yet.

Never give up on yourself. Methodologies will change. Technologies will change. Organizations will change. The specific tools and frameworks and platforms that defined your career at one point will be superseded by new ones, and the new ones will eventually be superseded in turn. What does not change is you: the judgment you have built, the relationships you have cultivated, the character you have developed through the work of doing hard things in complex environments over a long period of time. That travels. That compounds. That is yours.

Find a job that isn't a job. Find work that you love enough that the hard days are still worth it, that the invisible days are still satisfying, that the early mornings and the long migrations and the hundredth time you have explained the same thing to a new leader are still, somewhere underneath the fatigue, meaningful. That is not a luxury. Genuine engagement is the only sustainable strategy for a long career.

• • •

The clock will keep moving. People will come and go. Programs will be funded and cut and rebuilt. Administrations will change. Industries will shift. The landscape of work in the next decade will look different from the landscape of the last one in ways that none of us can fully predict.

Through all of it: you'll have yourself. Your family. Your friends. The people who believed in you before you fully believed in yourself, and the people you will believe in before they believe in themselves. The work you love enough to keep doing. The skills you keep building because you are genuinely curious about what comes next.

That is enough. That has always been enough.

• • •

Somewhere right now, in a production booth or a program office or a home office or a co-working space, someone is doing the unseen work. Running the ceremonies that nobody attends if they go well. Managing the vendor relationship that never makes it into the executive summary. Keeping the system up so that the people who depend on it never have to think about their dependence on it. Writing the documentation that someone will read in two years when the person who wrote it is long gone. Building the thing that will outlast the budget cycle that almost killed it.

That person is you. That has always been you. And I want you to know—even when the room doesn't know your name, even when the lights come up and the audience never looks back to see who called the cues, that the work you are doing is real, and it matters, and somewhere in the background of every great moment someone made it possible.

The unseen professional shows up.

Every single time.

Key Concepts

The following are the core ideas and frameworks introduced throughout this book. They are gathered here as a quick reference—not as a substitute for the chapters themselves, but as a reminder of the language and thinking the book is built around.

The Unseen Professional

The Product Manager, program lead, or enterprise practitioner who does the essential work that makes large organizations function—without appearing in the program notes. Not a failure of recognition, but a description of the role: the person whose best work is visible in outcomes, not in credit. The conductor who makes the orchestra possible but whose name most audience members never think to ask.

The Rulemaker Relationship

In large regulated organizations, the people who write policy and interpret compliance requirements are not obstacles. They are stakeholders with legitimate authority and real operational constraints. Building genuine relationships with rulemakers before you need something from them is one of the highest-leverage investments an enterprise Product Manager can make. The rulemaker who knows you will almost always treat you differently than the rulemaker who is hearing from you for the first time in a crisis.

Compliance as a Feature

Regulatory and governance requirements in large organizations are not external constraints imposed on the product. They are part of what the product is. A platform that meets Section 508 accessibility standards is a better platform. A system that passes a security audit is a more trustworthy system. Treating compliance as a feature means building it into the product from the beginning rather than bolting it on at the end, and means understanding that the rulemakers who enforce it are protecting something real.

The 95/5 Rule

Ninety-five percent of users need ninety-five percent of the features, reliably and well. Five percent of users need edge-case functionality that can consume a disproportionate share of development time and complexity. The discipline of enterprise product management is knowing which requests belong to the ninety-five and which belong to the five, and building decision-making structures that keep the five from driving the roadmap at the expense of the ninety-five. The five percent is not unimportant. Credentials are just not the foundation.

The Lily Pad Career

A career built not on a straight line toward a predetermined destination, but on a series of deliberate leaps from one solid platform to the next, each one made possible by the one before it. The lily pad model reframes non-linear career paths as a strength rather than a liability. Skills accumulated in one role become the foundation for the next. The flight dispatcher becomes the technical director becomes the federal IT specialist becomes the enterprise Product Manager. None of it was wasted. All of it traveled.

The Translation Toolkit

The set of skills that allows an enterprise practitioner—particularly one moving from government or regulated environments into the private sector, to make their experience legible to audiences who lack the reference points to evaluate it directly. Translation is not exaggeration or reframing. The translation is finding the private sector analog for the public sector reality: the $35 million portfolio, the 9,000-user platform, the multi-vendor coordination. The capability is real. The burden of making it visible belongs to the person who has it.

The Silent Ninja

The practitioner who solves problems before they become visible, who removes obstacles before they become blockers, who makes the hard things look easy through preparation and deliberate invisibility. Coined by a colleague in Minnesota and carried through two decades of professional life. The silent ninja does not need to be seen doing the work. The work being done is enough.

The Orchestra Model

A framework for understanding the enterprise Product Manager's relationship to their team and their organization. The infrastructure team is the double bass: rarely noticed, essential to everything. Senior developers are the first violins. Junior developers the second. Business analysts the violas. UX designers the woodwinds. The Scrum Master is the concertmaster: the bridge between conductor and ensemble. The help desk is percussion—invisible until something goes wrong. The Product Manager is the conductor: the one person in the room whose job is to hear everything at once and make it cohere. Not the loudest instrument. Not the most technically demanding. The one that makes all the others possible.

Further Reading

The following books have shaped how I think about leadership, communication, human behavior, and organizational dynamics. They are not a comprehensive curriculum—they are the ones I have actually read and returned to. Each one changed something about how I approach the work. Where relevant, I have noted the chapters in this book where each one connects most directly.

On Leadership and Influence

Turn the Ship Around!—L. David Marquet

The most honest book about leading without positional authority I have encountered. Marquet took command of the worst-performing submarine in the US Navy and turned it into the best—not by giving better orders, but by dismantling the order-giving model entirely. His concept of moving authority to the information, rather than moving information to the authority, is the intellectual foundation of almost everything described in Chapter Nine and Chapter Ten. If the phrase "influence without authority" has ever frustrated you because it tells you what to do without telling you how, this book fills that gap.

How to Win Friends and Influence People—Dale Carnegie

Still the foundation after nearly ninety years. Carnegie's core insight—that people are moved by feeling genuinely understood, not by being argued with or impressed—sits underneath every stakeholder conversation, vendor relationship, and executive briefing in this book. Chapter Two on the rulemaker relationship, Chapter Eleven on the 115 briefings, and Chapter Nine on influence without authority are all, in some sense, applied Carnegie. The language is dated in places. The principles are not.

The 6 Types of Working Genius—Patrick Lencioni

A short, practical framework for understanding why certain kinds of work energize some people and drain others—and why teams built without attention to that variation struggle to sustain momentum across a full product lifecycle. Lencioni identifies six types of work that every initiative requires: Wonder, Invention, Discernment, Galvanizing, Enablement, and Tenacity. Most people are naturally strong in two or three and frustrated by others. Relevant to Chapter Ten on coaching team members toward their natural strengths, and to Chapter Six on building Agile teams that can actually go the distance.

On Reading People and Rooms

StandOut—Marcus Buckingham

A framework for understanding your natural strengths—not the kind you have learned through effort, but the kind that come so easily you barely notice them. Buckingham's StandOut assessment identifies nine strength roles, and the results have a way of explaining patterns in your career that you have felt but never quite named. Relevant to Chapter Ten on coaching and to the broader question of building a career around what you are wired to do rather than what you think you should be good at. If you have not taken the assessment, the book includes access. The results are worth sitting with.

What Every Body Is Saying—Joe Navarro

A former FBI counterintelligence agent's guide to nonverbal communication—what people's bodies reveal about what they are thinking and feeling, independent of what they are saying out loud. This book is directly applicable to every situation in Part Three where reading the room matters more than reading the agenda: the executive briefing where the decision has already been made, the vendor meeting where something is being withheld, the stakeholder conversation where the stated concern is not the real one. If you have ever sensed that something was off without being able to name it, Navarro gives you the vocabulary and the discipline to trust what you are observing.

Blink—Malcolm Gladwell

An exploration of how experts make fast, accurate judgments—and when to trust that instinct and when to examine it more carefully. Less rigorous than Navarro but more readable, and useful for thinking about the kind of pattern recognition that accumulates over a long career in a complex environment. The experience described in Chapter Eleven—of being able to answer hard questions about an eight-year program without needing to look anything up—is what Gladwell is trying to explain. Worth reading alongside What Every Body Is Saying for a fuller picture of what it means to read a situation well.

On Careers and the Long Game

Range—David Epstein

The counterargument to the ten-thousand-hours theory of expertise, and the most validating book I have found for anyone who has taken a non-linear path through their career. Epstein makes a compelling, research-backed case that breadth of experience produces a different and in many contexts more valuable kind of capability than early specialization—that the generalist who has moved across domains brings a pattern-matching ability that deep specialists often lack. Chapter Fifteen on the pivot and the Introduction's lily pad model are both better understood alongside this book. If you have ever wondered whether the detours cost you something, Epstein's answer is almost certainly no.

So Good They Can't Ignore You—Cal Newport

A direct challenge to the follow-your-passion framework for career development, and the book I wish I had read earlier. Newport argues that passion follows mastery rather than the other way around—that the satisfaction and meaning people associate with their best work is usually the result of becoming genuinely excellent at something over time, not of finding the right fit at the beginning. The career described in Chapter Fifteen—built incrementally, through deliberate skill accumulation rather than destination-seeking—is exactly the kind of career Newport is describing. Pairs naturally with Range: Epstein explains why breadth has value, Newport explains how depth gets built.

On Enterprise Product and Technology

Inspired—Marty Cagan

The standard reference for product management practice, and worth reading specifically for its treatment of the gap between output and outcome—between shipping features and delivering actual value to users. Cagan writes primarily about technology companies rather than government or regulated enterprise environments, which means some translation is required, but the core discipline he describes maps directly onto the roadmap and backlog work in Chapters Four and Five. His chapters on continuous discovery align closely with the user research practices described in Chapter Eight.

The Phoenix Project—Gene Kim, Kevin Behr, and George Spafford

Fiction, and the more useful for it. The most accurate portrayal of enterprise IT dysfunction—and of how product and DevOps thinking eventually resolves it—that I have found in any format. The fictional IT director at the center of the story will be recognizable to anyone who has managed a large platform through a crisis, a leadership transition, or a compliance audit. Read it alongside Chapter Twelve on when things break and Chapter Six on Agile in the real world. You will recognize people from your own organization on almost every page, which is either reassuring or unsettling depending on which character they most resemble.

About the Author

Nathaniel Dull is a Senior Product Manager with more than ten years of experience leading enterprise technology programs in complex, regulated environments. He spent a decade at the Centers for Medicare and Medicaid Services, where he managed a SharePoint portfolio serving 9,000 users across one of the largest federal agencies in the United States—overseeing a $35 million contract portfolio, coordinating 120 vendor team members, and delivering more than 2,000 projects with a 95 percent on-time completion rate. He holds SAFe Product Owner/Product Manager (POPM) and Professional Scrum Master II (PSM II) certifications, and has deep hands-on experience with cloud-native platforms including Google Cloud Platform and Kubernetes.

After leaving federal service, Nathaniel joined a pharmacy benefits management company, where he leads product strategy for a containerized clinical application built on GCP and Google Kubernetes Engine. His career has spanned audio-visual production, federal contracting, information security, and enterprise product leadership—each chapter building on the last in ways that were rarely obvious at the time.

Outside of work, Nathaniel is a licensed private pilot and a devoted husband and father of two daughters.

Connect with him on LinkedIn at linkedin.com/in/nathaniel-dull/ or visit his website at nathanieldull.com.

Acknowledgments

This book would not exist without the people who shaped the career it describes. My father, whose decades in technology taught me what it looks like to build things from the ground up. My mother, who was always there in the background—steady, supportive, and present in the way that only becomes fully visible when you stop to look. The mentors at the church in Minnesota where I first learned to lead under pressure. The executive producer in Chicago who showed me that calm is a skill. The colleagues and leaders at CMS who trusted me with programs that mattered and gave me room to grow inside them.

And my wife—my biggest supporter, the person who has made it possible for me to pursue the things I want to pursue while we build something together that matters more than any of it: a family, two remarkable daughters, and a life that has room for continuous improvement and the kind of love that makes the lily pad jumps feel less terrifying than they would otherwise be.

www.ingramcontent.com/pod-product-compliance
Lightning Source LLC
LaVergne TN
LVHW022208200926
848481LV00006B/1895